The Trail of the Seed of the Woman

A Walk Through Genesis

Volume 2

Mike Potts

Library of Congress Control Number: 2019906586

ISBN: 978-0-9977477-9-9

First Printing: July 2019

Published by: 102nd Place, LLC
Scottsdale, AZ

Table of Contents

Introduction

Volume 1 of *The Trail of the Seed of the Woman* closed
with Abraham trusting completely in God's word. We
take up Volume 2 with the next generation of "Seed
Transporters." There's to be a bride for Isaac, who will
bring about the birth of twin boys. One trouble will lead
to the next, yet we'll see as in the first volume that God
brings about His purpose. He restores the characters in
His-Story who mess their lives up with sin time and time
again. He brings about the family who will, in turn,
become the 12 tribes of Israel. One tribe, in particular,
the Tribe of Judah, will be the one in which the "Seed of
the Woman" will come forth. He will be called the Lion
of Judah, our Lord, and Savior. The prophecy given to
Abraham in Chapter 15 would indeed turn into the large
family who would end up in Egypt and become slaves
for 400 years. God said this would come to pass, and it
did. We will see that it started here in Genesis.

In this volume of His-Story, we will find that a large part
centers on Jacob and his challenges. Then on to Joseph
and his brother's hatred; selling Joseph into slavery
which God has planned. He will turn this around for the
good of the family whom God will use to carry the "Seed
of the Woman." The "seed" will eventually pay our debt
of sin on the Cross.

To me, it's an exciting story full of suspense that God
keeps His characters in till the end. Again, as I stated in
the first volume, it's a lesson of Faith and Confidence in

God for us that He will carry us through to Himself as He promised us in Christ. (Romans 15:4)

What I hope and try to declare to you of our Sovereign God is: for From Him, and Through Him, and To Him are all things, to Whom be the Glory for Ever. Amen!

As in Volume 1, I encourage you to use your Bible to search out the verses I reference to validate that what I am telling you is correct. Following most of the chapters, there will be a few questions to think on that I hope help you apply this study to your lives.

Blessings,

Mike Potts

An Honorable Woman of God Dies; a Family Cemetery is Bought; This is Home!

Howdy, it's mornin' here in AZ. Gonna be a nice day, thank you, Lord! In Volume 1, we got through the high point in Abraham's life. God commended his Faith to a tough command, blessed him, and then Abe goes back to his life's routine as a herdsman. Isaac is now a man and the end of the life of Abe's wife Sarah comes.

Let's pray.

Genesis 23:1–20 KJV

I. Sarah, the Mother of Nations and Kings.

A. Verses 1 and 2. While we look back over her life, yes, there were stains of error in her thinking and faith. But also, there were those qualities of a Godly woman in her that God recognized and commended her for later in the New Testament.

1. 1 Peter 3:6. God recognized that Sarah submitted to her husband to where she called him Lord and obeyed him. God used her as an example for women to follow as well as with actions in 1 Peter 3:1–5.
2. Hebrews 11:11. God says, "She through faith in God's word," received strength to conceive and delivered a child when she was past the age. So,

while she didn't start out well suggesting Abe take Hagar, yet in time, her faith grew by Grace. Likewise, we should take her as an example and not stay in our failures or see other's failures, BUT hope in God!

B. Verse 1. She is now 127-years-old, so that means Isaac is 37-years-old. God had given her a gift of making her body young and strong enough, as well as her womb open to conceive, give birth, and to nurse. But that later faded away till now we see her appointed time had come. She dies in Hebron. Verse 2

1. This verse also says Abe "came to mourn for Sarah." Where was he? Perhaps in Beersheba by his well, overseeing part of their herd while Sarah was in Hebron. I don't know, but he seems to be away from her when she died.
2. Abraham God did personally Bless with wealth. Not only were his herds vast, but he also had many servants as well as much riches. Likewise, God gave those in the land of Canaan understanding that Abe's God was powerful and protected Abe. Remember he and Mamre with their men followed the kings of the east and took back all they'd taken from those around the Dead Sea and rescued Lot. Then Abimelech learned to fear Abe and his God and knew Abe was a Prophet of God. (Chapter 20) Abe's family was respected and even feared in the Land of Canaan. He was recognized as a Great Man. So likewise, many of the people of that region came to pay their respects to this Lady – Sarah. One other thing I forgot, this woman who was old, became young enough to have a child and live long enough to see him become a man. This would cause her, as well as

Abe, to be a wonder to behold! So, Sarah was well known 21:6–7, "so that all that hear will laugh with me" – rejoiced with me the people of the land. They recognized Abe and Sarah were special, even though these neighbors weren't Children of God.

   3. Abraham loved and missed her and wept for her.

II. Abraham needs some land in which to bury his family.

   A. These Sons of Ham, many of whom were of leadership rank, were there to give respect to Abe and his wife. Verse 3. Abe stood up from his grief. He knew he needed something recognizable to mark that this land was his and his future family's, as ordained by God. (Even though the people of Canaan don't know this.)

     1. Verse 4 starts by saying the truth, "I am a stranger, and a sojourner." We can refer here again to Hebrews 11:9–10, then 13–16 explains the thinking of Abraham at this point. He did not intend to go back to his "birthplace" claiming that as home. God has already had Abe make the "covenant circumcision" that signifies the sanctification or separation from the people of the land. Therefore, among the people of this land a stranger, yet the land is going to be his Seed's by the right of God to give to whom He wills to give. (Deuteronomy 9:5–6) This wealthy man lived in a tent traveling with his herd, following the good grass and water, but as a "sojourner" in the above verses. It explains he had an expectation that his permanent home is in eternity with His, and our, Lord and Savior.

     2. In verses 4 through16, Abe knows this land will be his "Seed's" land by the right and word of God, yet he insists on paying a fair price for a burial

plot. Those at the funeral respected him and offered to give him what he wanted for free. But he knew it had to be bought for a fair price to be recognized that this land is now their home in this world. He knew the piece of land he wanted; it had trees as well as open land looking out on his old friend Mamre's country, and a rocky hill from which a grave could be hollowed out. In verse 16, we see the land was paid for in front of witnesses.

3. This ceremony happened in the "Gate of the City" Hebron, where, back then, all things of importance happened. Verse 10. This was an area that had a city on it by the same name. While this place was called "Canaan," there were several other people groups besides Canaanites through the region. Hittites were mainly in what is now called Turkey, but they were throughout Canaan as well. Ephron was a Hittite. Ephron offered a price, and Abe didn't try to bring the price down; just measured it out in silver and bought it. The land was bought in front of many witnesses. The land now is his in which not only Sarah will be buried, but also Abe, Isaac, Rebecca, Leah, and Jacob.

III. The land bought and paid for is now recognized as Abraham's.

A. Verses 17 and 18 make it clear the land is Abe's.

B. In verse 19, Abe attends to the burial of his dear wife, Sarah.

C. Verse 20. Again, it states that the people of that land confirmed this plot of land is Abraham's possession as a burying place "by the Sons of Heth."

1. Today the City of Hebron has expanded out past Ol' Abe's land, and there is a Muslim Mosque over the place. (They too claim Abe as their father through Ol' Ish. I understand we can't go in there without a fight (being we ain't Muslims.)

This all went down according to His-Story. He molded these people into the men and women He wanted them to be and worked through them despite themselves, as He does through you and me. We're all like grass, here for a while, then in full bloom, then withered and dead. If we hope in this life, our Hope is in vain. Thank God for Grace and the confidence we have through Christ's Resurrection!

Scott C. Thanks for that word of encouragement this morning!

Questions for Discussion

1. Instead of staying in our failures or dwelling on other's failures, what should we do?
2. Do you understand how Deuteronomy 9:5–6 applies to us as well? Why?

The Lord of Hosts has Sworn.
Therefore, We Have Assurance

Mornin' folks. Gonna try and get this study out by Thursday. We're flying to Alaska to help out with the grandkids Friday. So, we saw in the last study Sarah has gone home to the Lord, Abe's getting old, and the focus now is on the next "seed transporter," Isaac. We're going to see faith in action by Abe, Abe's servant is going to learn to trust God, see His testing request answered, and God's purpose revealed.

Let's pray.

Genesis 24:1–27 KJV

I. Abe is old, but God has Blessed him, and now Abe will follow God's plan for His Seed, a wife for Isaac.

A. Verse 1. As we saw last week, God blessed Abraham with wealth in herds, servants (he had an army of his own), and riches. Blessed in all things.

B. We need to remember just because we are not told everything exactly that God told Abraham, doesn't mean when Abe says things like he is about to, that he's just guessing what to do. He's going to request that no wife will come from Canaan for Isaac (verse 3) because God told him that.

   1. Here in verse 2, Abe tells Eliezer, his head servant,

"Put . . . thy hand on my thigh." What Abe's saying is they take oath giving seriously. He's telling Eliezer, grab my crotch. They were not too shy back then, and they were straight shooters. The idea is one of two possibilities. First, if ya break your vow to me even though I'm old, my "seed" will take vengeance on you. Or second, the fact that God had them circumcised as a sign of separation from pagans and set apart to God. Therefore, by that, the oath was made. Eliezer was to go get a bride for Isaac from Abe's hometown people; really from his own family. Verse 4.

2. Then in verses 5 and 6, Eliezer asks a good question that Abe answers. If a girl won't come with me, do I have to come back here, get Isaac and go again? To which Abe answers, nope, Isaac is never to leave this land that God has given us as an inheritance.

3. In verse 7, we see the faith Abraham has in God's word. So, paraphrasing: "even though Eliezer, this that I'm asking you, humanly thinking, looks questionable and tuff, I know what God, Jehovah-jireh, intends and therefore, it will be provided. I trust Him to prepare the way. He will send Angels ahead so who He intends for Isaac to marry will be ready for you to find and bring back here." (Who we know is Rebekah, verses 8 and 9.) "But, Eliezer, if I'm wrong, you are clear of your sworn obligation to me." So, Eliezer grabs Abe's crotch and swears to do this tuff thing. He's gonna travel over 500 miles and back again with a small army (which was needed for protection in those days) and ten camels carrying riches of gold and silver plus grub and camp for the trip. Verse 10. (I've been there, done that. Ya gotta have a good outfit.) Eliezer's gonna learn a thing or two about God

that we all need to learn. Mesopotamia and the city of Nahor are where Iraq is today on the other side of the Euphrates river and a far bit north of that river.

II. So Eliezer has journeyed to Nahor. Now what, God?

A. We come to verses 11 to 14. Eliezer has obeyed. He's traveled to where his master has told him to go but isn't sure what to do next. So, he calls on the one who was to have all this organized, God. Basically, he asks God to bring the girl to him. He knows this is the right time for women to get their water. He petitions God to make the right girl known to him by having her give himself and his camels water. In this way, he will know his master's God is the true God, and all his master said about his God is true and can be trusted with whatever his God commands.

1. The answer verses 15 and 16 – amazing! I'm thinkin' Eliezer thought it's gonna take a long time to search out the girl that Abraham was talkin' about who God had appointed. Could this be her? The first girl we've come across? Let's read on and see, remembering the request Eliezer made.

2. Verses 17 through 27. Everything that Eliezer asked came to pass! God led him directly to where he would meet the right girl that the Lord God of Abraham intended for Isaac! When you think on this, why would we doubt that God would? Likewise, when God intends for a certain plan for us to be, why do we think like Eliezer, that this may be difficult? Abe knew by experience God would provide (Jehovah-jireh), while Eliezer was still in the learning process, as I am. But as we see here, that is about to change. Notice verse 21, is this the

girl? Eliezer is watching her water his camels, then takes gold earrings and bracelets and gives them to her. At this point, he asks the important question, "So who's your family and would there be room for us for the night?" Verse 23.

III. Eliezer learns what God intends to be He will provide.

A. Rebekah answers, verses 24 and 25. God has organized everything to happen just the way He intended. This is the girl that he was looking for!

1. Verses 26 and 27. Eliezer responds. He worships the God of Abraham, who Abraham declared in verse 3, I will make you swear by the God who made the Heavens and the Earth. Therefore, declaring the only True God. This is who Eliezer is worshiping now. Verse 27. He speaks to the depth of his realization, what God says, will be! God didn't leave Abe his master without what He promised, the continuation of "The Seed of the Woman." He is amazed God led him right to "the house of my master's brethren!" This lesson is what Romans 15:4 is referring to for us. What God says we can Trust!

Well, that's a good place to stop and for us to think on. Blessings to ya, Mike

Questions for Discussion

1. Put yourself in Eliezer's shoes. He's traveled over 500 miles in tuff weather. Ya get tired too. Then ya wonder; will I find her? You're probably a believer in Christ if you're reading this. How

would your faith be? Read 1 Corinthians 10:12. I'd have to say I don't know, but God, meaning He would get us through! Admitting weakness is the first step to experience that God's Will, will be done. (2 Corinthians 12:9)

We Begin a New Chapter in His-Story

Howdy, folks. We're in Fairbanks, Alaska watchin' the grandkids awhile. Jody's helping train new recruits into VPSO program (village cops) down in Sitka, AK. Well, we saw last study that Eliezer discovered what Abe had already. When God declares what He intends to happen and sends us on a mission that seems humanly risky at best to impossible at worst, His command will be accomplished in us. We can trust His word and GO! Eliezer is amazed as he prayed the request to God, even before he finished, the right girl came and did as he requested. It took God to make this happen, to recognize the right girl. So, he's to bring her to his master's son for a wife. Now Eliezer will meet Rebekah's family.

Let's pray.

Genesis 24:28–67 KJV

A. Verses 28 to 33 tell about the meeting, and we're introduced to a character that will play an important part in Jacob's life, the next "Seed Transporter." Laban, the brother of Rebekah, who will later be a trickster to Jacob and have him put in 14 years hard labor. This so Jacob could end up marrying Laban's younger daughter, the one he wanted, but first marrying the older daughter, the one he didn't want. Anyway, we'll get to that later. But for now, Laban is excited and runs out to meet this mystery man who comes from his long-lost uncle, Abe. We need to stop here a minute and reflect on God's purpose for the Line from which Jesus the Christ will come. Early on, we saw in Genesis 9:26 that it will be in the line of or the "Seed" of SHEM. They will be the people that are special to God, set apart from other people, from whom the Savior will come. At this point, God wants to keep this line pure, no Canaanites just Shemites. This is why all the trouble to go back to Haran and to Abe's family's house. Later we'll see a Moabite woman named Ruth will be in the line. But really if you remember, they were Shemites too through Lot, but they probably didn't worry about keeping the line pure. Also, in the book of Joshua, we meet Rahab the whore, who's a Canaanite. She will be in our Savior's line. She will be the mother of Boaz who will marry the Moabite woman Ruth. Also, Tamar was a Hamite who Judah, the son of Jacob, fathered a son that the "Seed of the Woman" continued in through his son, Pharez. But for now, at the start of the "Seed Transporters," God wants the Line to be PURE SHEM. So, let's break down this meeting the family of Rebekah's with Eliezer.

1. Rebekah runs back and tells her family of meeting this strange man who gave her expensive jewelry and that her uncle Abe had sent to find them. Verses 28 and 30.
2. They're excited and send Laban, Rebekah's brother to go check this guy out, and welcome Eliezer to come to their home. Verses 29 and 31.
3. So, Eliezer and his band of merry men come to Bethuel's house and are taken care of right down to their tired feet and hungry camels. (They were obviously rich cause there's a lot of mouths with Eliezer to feed and care for!) Verse 32.
4. They set the food before their guests, but Eliezer can't wait to tell them of his mission and how God answered him and led him to them and says,

"Thanks, but I just gotta tell ya all what God did before I eat anything!" Verse 33.

5. From verse 34 down to 48, he recites everything that was, and is, and knows the things that will come. For now, he knows what God's word is: Un-concealed Reality – TRUTH and praises the God of his master, who now is his God. Verse 48.

II. Bethuel recognizes God's calling on Rebekah and gives his daughter to Isaac.

A. After reciting the God-led events, Eliezer asks, "So, can I take her or what?" Verse 49.

B. Verses 50 and 51. It says Laban and Bethuel answered, so it appears Laban had some influence on family matters along with his father. Anyway, the upshot was: "Yep, the God of Abraham has chosen our girl, and whether we like it or not, she should go to Isaac. Take her and go".

C. Again Eliezer is amazed! Man, this gettin' a wife for my master's son is a cake walk! God had everything planned out perfectly! (Why should we be surprised? Yet we often have short, dumb spells and doubt! Oh! Us of little Faith!)

1. Verse 52. He kneels down and worships God. Then as a gift to the bride's family, he lays out the riches that Abe gave him to give to Rebekah, and then what to me is interesting, it says here also gave to her brother and mother but not poor ole' Bethuel. Interesting and it doesn't give an explanation as to why either. One commentator

thinks it was proof their daughter will be well taken care of.

D. Verse 54. Here it points to what I mentioned early on that Eliezer had a small army traveling with him for protection and help with the camel train (and the men that were with him). He now eats the food that was brought before him.

1. And at that time tells Laban and Bethuel, "I want to get goin' home right away so I can get this responsibility over with."
2. Verses 55 to 59. They tell him, "Ah, don't be in a hurry. Give us a few days to get used to the idea she's leavin' us. Her ma's gonna cry a lot." But Eliezer can't wait to get this whole thing over with and is persistent. They say, "Well, we'll leave it up to sister if she wants to go right away or not." Rebekah comes out, and they ask her, and she says, "Let's get goin'!" So, it's settled. The bride for Isaac is on the way! Verse 59.
3. Verse 60. The family Blessing on their little girl. It's obvious they see God's design in all this in what they say next: "Be thou the mother of thousands of millions, and let thy seed possess the gates of those which hate them." (Interesting twist – which hate them?) The N.A.S. and N.I.V. versions of the Bible both use cities instead of gates, which is still pointing to the taking of Canaan, as God had ordained. But here it says, "of those who hate you." The whole world hates not only Jesus but us and Israel as well. God may have used Rebekah's family in a prophetic announcement about the millennial reign of Christ along with Israel. Whether that includes the whole church or not, is debated by those who

come to Bible study as Dispensationalist or Reformed. (Galatians 6:15–16 King James version.) But anyway, we know what has passed. Israel owns the land promised to Abraham (even when they are absent to that land). This whole thing is interesting later when Jacob comes here to Laban, who appears to be a pagan still. (Genesis 31:19, 30,32,35)

4. Verse 61. So, Rebekah left with her maids-in-waiting and rode a camel following Eliezer. He probably resupplied with grub and water and things of Rebekah's. Eliezer is probably relieved "to put on the big skedaddle" home before anyone changes their mind. (Not that they would cause God is behind this.)

III. Here comes Da Bride! Also, this is an example of Christ and His Bride.

A. Verses 62 and 63. Isaac is in his home country caring for what God has given him and waiting for whom God has prepared for him. John 14:3.

1. Lahai-roi is probably the well where Hagar first met the Lord who then sent her back to Sarai. The meaning is interesting: the well of the Living One who sees me. But this is where Isaac is waiting for his bride.

2. If ya read verse 65 first, it's clearer then verse 64 (to me anyway). Revelations 19:7; 21:9. The Holy Spirit in Romans 8:26–27 comes to mind as Eliezer explains to Rebekah about Isaac and later to Isaac about Rebekah, and how God led him to Rebekah. Verse 66.

B. The Wedding – verse 67 and Revelations 21:9; then the Marriage, Ephesians 5:23–32.

1. She veiled herself at their first meeting so that only the eyes could be seen which was the custom.
2. Notice verse 62. Isaac Came From. The meeting was in the area where part of the family's herds where grazing and some of their herdsmen were camped there. Isaac took her to his mother's tent. When he first saw her unveiled, he sparked like the Fourth of July. The marriage was consummated; they became one.
3. "Was comforted after his mother's death." (Genesis 2:24) Also, the idea in Genesis 2:20, where man saw that living alone makes one realize there's something missing in one's life. Then God took care of the problem with Eve, as He planned, but wanted Adam to realize he had a need (besides God) to be whole. Verse 23. Then verse 24 is what was the plan of the Author of Life making man whole.

So again, God's amazing story and the Trail of the Seed of the Woman continues. Next, we'll see Abe heading to a city not made by hands and leaves the promised "Seed" behind. Hebrews 11:10,16.

Blessings, to ya all! Mike

Questions for Discussion

1. Does the Holy Spirit play a bigger role in our lives than you or I realize?
2. In these volumes 1 and 2, I often say His-Story. Do you see God orchestrating His-Story exactly

as He intends?

3. What should that do for our faith? In Romans 15:4, the word Hope could probably be better understood as Confidence.

Good Bye, Abe. See Ya There!

Mornin' from Alaska. Abe's gonna leave us now. God did some amazing things through him. After celebrating Abe's life here and recognizing all his kids and wives, we'll look at Ol' Ish's offspring and Abe's sons through his second marriage. Then we'll move into following Isaac and his family. All that in one chapter.

Let's pray.

Genesis 25:1–18 KJV

I. Before Abe dies, but after Sarah's death, he marries again. Or was Sarah still alive?

A. That's a good question. When did Keturah come into Abe's life? Some commentators in their study seem to think that it's more probable that Keturah was a concubine prior to Sarah's death, not after, while others think that it was after. The differing thinking seems to center around how long a period did Abe stay young enough (the Gift of God making his body young enough to have children) to sire offspring? The simple answer to that is, who knows! Verse 6 calls both Hagar and Keturah concubines, as does 1 Chronicles 1:32. As I've found out, investigating something that went on a few decades ago, when asking an Ol' timer who was there, usually it ends up somewhat different than I thought or the evidence seemed to show. Likewise, in the Bible. Often times, the Bible is just a summary of what went on. Issues like this, we can only guess at, or just say not sure when, or just what all was going on. One thing that struck me as interesting is that when Sarah died, Abe wasn't there. Verses 23:2; 24:62,67. It was Sarah's tent, not Abe's or Isaac's. Seems from 22:19 Abe was near his well in Beersheba. All these details don't take away from the important event we need to keep our focus on, the fact that Isaac was a miracle of God meant to continue the line of our Savior. It's interesting to speculate on (or maybe it's gossip). Nonetheless, God didn't seem to have a problem with Jacob having two wives and two concubines and later the Kings of Israel. So, who knows when or what all went down? Nonetheless, she, Keturah, bore him six sons.

1. Zimran, Jokshan, Medan, Midian, Ishbak, and Shuah. But, only two of the sons were mentioned, Jokshan and Midian. Why? I don't know, but the next two verses (3, 4) list them. These were the sons that Abraham had by Keturah. These, along with the sons of Ishmael, are who became the Arabs, from whom Mohamed and Islam would come later.

2. Verses 5 and 6. As expected, most all that Abraham had stayed with Isaac in the PROMISED LAND with the PROMISED SON from Sarah. The rest of his children he wanted to be separated from Isaac so things wouldn't get complicated or compromised concerning the purity of the Line, His chosen people. So, all the rest of his sons he sent east with plenty for them to continue their present lifestyle as herdsmen. They had to have enough animals not only for their immediate family but also for servants who were capable of fighting if need be: warriors. Abe's wealth was VAST! We need to remember this for it wasn't

safe to wander off with much wealth, whether herds or gold or both. Might was right back then. If you couldn't protect what you had, plan on losing it real quick! So again, these sons populated what is known as the Arabian Peninsula intermixed with others that became known as Arabs.

II. Then He Dies

A. Verses 7 and 8. Abraham lived for 175 years, which even back then was old. Notice it says in verse 8, "was gather to his people." I think we need to remember back to Genesis 3:15 where God said basically there will be two types of people; those of the World starting with Cain, and those who are not of this world, but passing through this world. The phrase I'm referring to is, "and between thy seed (talking to Satan his seed are those of the world, see John 15:18–19) and her seed." These are those God has elected to be Born-Again and in faith of God's promised Savior. Therefore, those that He's going to be gathered to Him will be not his earthly family, but those Chosen of God out of this world like Noah, etc. Jump ahead to Luke 16:22 and Galatians 3:6–7. As we know, the Elect will be with Abraham.

1. Isaac and Ishmael seem to have straightened out their differences and worked together to bury their father. Verse 9. And sounds like the wishes of their father were respected. He was buried next to his wife, Sarah, in their family burial plot, recognizing this was the land God has given His chosen people, which will be Israel. Verse10.
2. Verse 11. Isaac is now a married man and the only "Seed Transporter" alive. He goes to the well where Hagar saw the Lord for the first time (we mentioned that it seemed to be where he

liked to graze his herd in the last study). Lahai-roi, Genesis16:14, and in that area he's gonna hang his hat most of the time.

III. We will look at Ishmael's seed now.

A. "These are the generations of Ishmael." He had twelve sons.
1. Let's look at what God told Hagar and Abe about the future of their son.
   a. 16:12. He'd be a wild man or literally a wild ass. They are hard to tame, but for some reason valued highly, so Ishmael would be respected even though he'd be warring with men on all sides of him. But as it says here in 25:18, he'd dwell in the presence of all his Brethren.
   b. 17:20. he'd be blessed and have much. Also, he'd have 12 sons – Princes.
   c. 21:13. God will raise a nation up through him.
   d. 21:20,21. He became an archer and lived in wild country and married a Hamite.
2. It appears here in 25 that what God said, it came to pass. The 12 sons had communities named after them as well as many herdsmen-type tribes. He wasn't too far away from his brother, and he could get there in time for the funeral. I'd say it all played out the way God said it would.
3. One thing I'm curious about; was Ishmael saved? Did he get gathered with Abe or with his physical brethren of this world? As you look back at Hagar, God seemed to keep tabs on them both and looked out for them. That doesn't mean they were saved I know, but it doesn't mean they weren't either.
4. Verse 17. He lived 137 years and died perhaps east of where Isaac lived.

5. Verse18. Havilah is in Saudi Arabia, north of Yemen. It sounds like he died with his family around him.

We'll stop there and next time get introduced to Isaac's family. As we see here, what God said earlier did happen. From this, we should, with confidence in His word, trust Him with our lives.

Blessings, Mike

Ya Got a Problem? Who ya Gonna Call? The Foolishness of Man

Howdy ya all. Back from Mexico. Adeline is back from Alaska. Let's see what we can get done on this study.

Let's pray.

Genesis 25:19–34 KJV

I. It's interesting how God doesn't always explain the waiting we do.

A. In this section of chapter 25 (verses 19,20), God goes over again what went on in the last few chapters. Isaac is a full-blood Shemite and takes a Shemite for a wife as God directed Abe. Now the family Abe left are called Syrians.

B. I'm sure Isaac is fully aware of God's purpose for him as a "Seed Transporter" yet here it is 20 years with Rebekah his wife and no kids. What's goin' on? It's interesting, in one place God told Abe what's going to happen to his Seed that will become a nation (15:13–16) and it exactly came to pass as He explained. The reason God gave Abe for why it would take so long was that the Amorites haven't gotten sinful enough yet and it will take them over 400 years before that will happen. Yet, here God keeps Isaac guessin' as to why don't I have a son yet, or when will I get a son? So, after 20 years, Isaac asks God when will I have a son? (Verse 26, Ike was 60-years-old.) Do I have to wait till I'm 100 like Ol' Pa? Verse 21. And it seems Rebekah almost immediately conceived. I know God has the date appointed when and where all are born, but it often seems that prayer is what starts things to happen. (Philippians 4:6; Acts 12:5; 1 Peter 5:7; 1 Thessalonians 5:17) It's interesting God has ordained or appointed all things to happen, yet He tells us to pray and request our needs and concerns. Those two FACTS seem to be in conflict, yet they're both in His word; therefore, both Truth. It does seem that there are many times after prayer; things turn to the positive that is needed. I think two things that God desires from and for us are:

1. When praying, we are participating with Him in His work. Our faith is in Him, we are professing His promises, as well as knowing our needs, and the needs of others are met by Him, and for direction from Him on what to do. John 17 is a good example of this.
2. I think Philippians 4:7 answers our need that praying fulfills through Jesus, always through the blood He shed for us. We ask in His name. He is our High Priest.

II. Two types of people are examples here; the Seed of the serpent, and the Seed of the woman. (Genesis 3:15)

A. With the conception, there were twins in Rebekah. Verse 22. The two brothers were fighting in her. It got so bad Rebekah sought the Lord with concern and probably fearing as to why or what was happening in her. The answer from God was there are two types of people in you.

1. The one brother will become Esau, later known as Edom (Red), and will be the father of the Edomites.
2. The second brother will be named Jacob. The meaning seems to be heel catcher or trickster, but God will later give him the name Israel. He is the father of the Nation of Israel.
3. Both Nations will hate the other. Once Israel moves to the promised land of Canaan, they will be at war, and generally, Israel will be Edom's master. The last part of verse 23 says, "two manner of people . . . and the one people will be stronger than the other people, and the Elder shall serve the Younger." This came to pass with King David. This was a prophecy. Edom never really was completely destroyed till after Jerusalem fell in 70 A.D. But when Israel moved on their land, they were either at war with Israel or controlled by Israel and later invaded by the Babylonians. The hatred was strong between the two nations. These two brothers fathered, as God told Rebekah they would, two different Nations, and this is what the struggle signified.

B. Verses 24 to 28. Here again, we see the sovereign Hand of God choosing our parts to play in His-Story. Two types of people. God chose Isaac, not Ishmael, Jacob, not Esau. This is an issue with many Christians, the choice of God as to whom He will give Mercy and who will stay in His Wrath.

1. We should understand from the beginning (Genesis 3:15), that God speaks of "the Seed of the serpent" as those whom God has ordained or appointed to be children of His wrath, (examples are seen in Jude 4; 1 Peter 2:8; Daniel 4:34,35).

This story of God's concerning Isaac's sons is understood and explained further in Malachi 1:2,4 and in Romans 9:10–13 (key in on verse 11). This I think possibly is the hardest for many to TRULY understand, that Grace is not of any works such as our choice. Here in verse 11, it could not be explained any clearer, "that the purpose of God's Election might STAND, not of works, but of Him that calleth." (Ephesians 2:9)

2. And the "Seed of the Woman," these are those God made and chose to receive His mercy and by Grace be saved.

3. Jacob and Esau are just examples of how God works with ALL people. It might be helpful to go over Deuteronomy 9:4–6. The idea we seem to forget (easily, because we all have the part of sin God calls "The Pride of Life") is, we're ALL a bunch of bad guys and if He wants to take from one bunch of bad guys and give to another bunch of bad guys it's HIS choice!

C. Verses 24 to 26. So, the nine months passed, and the twins were born. It appears these two rascals were competing for the first one to come out of momma and into the world. Esau came first, pretty hairy and red. That's interesting cause most Shemites are dark-haired, with well-tanned skin, so he was different. Then what is real interesting is Jacob came and grabbed ahold of Esau's ankle as if to say, "Ya ain't going without me even if I didn't come out first." This represents what will soon come to pass: the struggle for first place in the family. But God, we already know, has that taken care of that.

1. Isaac didn't have to wait till he was a 100-yr-old, but he was 60, about the time you'd expect to have grandchildren. He was 40 when he received

Rebekah for a wife. The word damsel in 24:14 seems to be a girl in adolescence. I'm guessin' 13 to 16-years-old, so that puts her in her mid-30's when the boys were born. The reason I point this out is Isaac is going to lie about her being his wife in the next chapter and fear for his life like Abe did, cause even in her old age she seems to be a looker like Sarah was. But we'll look at that when we get there.

2. So, the boys grew. Verse 27. Esau became a man who loved the freedom to go where he wanted, wander the land, and kill what he wanted to eat. He'd a made a good Mongol or Sioux Warrior. He was care-less. What I mean is he couldn't care less about the future. He lived for the moment's Glory, just for himself, no responsibility. (I one time resembled that remark, so I know a little what he was like.) While Jake was a man who wanted all that his father had and was a thinking, organized man who could take care and build the family's herds. He probably also knew of the promise from God as to what he was to inherit. Whether yet God was working in him to have a saving faith or not, I can't say, but we know Jake is of the Elect of God. He loved Jacob and hated Esau (one commentator said love means chosen, and hate means rejected.) Nonetheless, love isn't earned. God chooses what bad guy he will love or hate.

3. Verse 28. Isaac's favorite was Esau, his rugged, tuff older son. Rebekah's favorite was Jacob. Esau was a man's man. Isaac was pleased and impressed with Esau's abilities, while Jacob was Rebekah's baby. But beyond that, it appears God may have given Rebekah faith in what He said. "The older will serve the younger." In other

words, the Birthright will go to Jacob. I'm sure Isaac knew, but he still seems to have, as we'll see, some (like me) wayward leanings.

III. The Care-less versus the crafty Gold-digger.

A. Verses 29 to 34 tell a shameful story of the two brothers. We mentioned earlier their natural tendencies, and they show here. Apparently, Jake had part of the family herd out away from the rest of the family, and it was still a long way to the main camp. Esau ran onto "Starvin' Times" and was "froze fur meat" as the Ol' Mountain Men use ta say. He was plumb weak for food. So, he sees Jake cooking his supper and says, "I'm about to fall over. Feed me."

1. True to form, Jake the sly one took advantage of his brother's condition knowing how careless his brother was. He said, "Sell me your birthright for a bowl of these beans." Esau, the care-less, live for the moment one, said, "What is my birthright worth if I starve to death? OK, give me the beans!" But Jake, the sly one said, "NO! You swear to me you will give me your birthright first. So, the care-less one said, "OK, I swear it!" And to God, and my thinkin' too, Esau despised what normally was a double portion of Isaac's wealth. But above that, he showed he couldn't care less about anything of God. Esau reminds me of 1 Corinthians 2:14. Those Born once – the things of God mean nothing to them nor can they.
2. The beans were red in color, and he begged for some, and later in mocking or shaming

Esau, his name changed to Edom which is Red for sold his birthright for red beans (lentils really).

Well, that's about it for this study. I think there's a good example of a fallen man here we can identify with if we're honest. Thank God for Grace.

Blessings, Mike

Questions for Discussion

1. Let's think on what much of the church says: God loves everyone. Let's follow a trail of verses and ask that question again. John 3:16, "God so loved the world." Now go to Genesis 1:26. The world is referring to humanity, the apple of God's eye in all creation. You with me so far? Now go to Romans 9:10–21. Where does that trail lead concerning God's love?
2. Now, remember Deuteronomy 9:4–6 and Romans 3:10–20. Do any of us deserve to be loved by God?
3. What does Romans 9:11 tell us?

So Quickly We Forget and Try to Solve Our Fears on Our Own

Howdy, folks! Hope all you had a Blessed Resurrection Sunday. I was called to preach that Sunday so spent most of the study time last week building up the message God wanted. We'll get back into Genesis 26 this week and see how far we get.

Let's pray.

Genesis 26:1–15 KJV

I. A bad dry spell and God reminds Isaac of His Promise to Abraham and now to him, Isaac.

A. Verse 1. A lot of time has passed. Isaac was married when he was 40 to Rebekah. Had two sons, twins at 60. His father, Abe, died when Isaac was 75. So how old is he here? I don't know. Yet, at the end of chapter 25, verse 34, Esau was 40. So, somewhere between 75-years-old and 100, a drought happened. The one Abe went through was at least 120 years earlier. Right? We don't have as clear a record as far as a timeline for Isaac as we did for Abe but later a pretty good one for Jacob.

B. Verses 2 to 5. God meets with Isaac to reaffirm His Promises to his father and to keep him in the Promised Land. (Sojourn in this land verse 3.)
  1. "I will be with thee." God here says I am the one to trust in.

2. "I will Bless thee!" God has already blessed Isaac with what his father Abe had. He got most of the vast family herds, along with riches, a great camp outfit and many servants. God's meaning is, you will keep this, as well as I will multiply what you have and also what your children have.

3. "I will perform the Oath which I gave to your father, Abraham." Perform equals continue with an idea of a Decree: "It will be as I said." This goes back to the Oath, and God's oath can be trusted. (Isaiah 14:24)

4. Verse 4. Explains to Isaac, what I'm sure Abe told him or he heard it on Mt. Moriah, (Genesis 22:17) that his children way down the line will get this land, "these countries."

5. But then says again to Isaac directly that he is a transporter of "The Seed of the Woman" who will be the savior, Jesus the Christ . . . shall all nations on earth be blessed."

C. Verse 5. God says He's confirming the Covenant not because Isaac is a good guy but because his father was. (Not that grace was given because of the good works Abe did, otherwise it wouldn't be grace. Romans 11:5–6) But Abe, by God's enabling, had worthiness. He feared God. (Genesis 22:12,16) He doesn't seem as close to Isaac as to Abe for some reason. (But that may just be me.)

II. When fear gets ahold of you, Faith is left behind.

A. Verse 6. Gerar was in Philistine if ya remember from chapter 10. They were Hamites who, from Egypt, sailed to the Island of Crete, then later some came here even before Abe.

1. Verse 7. Back then these Shemite women must have aged VERY gracefully because Rebekah being about 25 years younger than Isaac, would be 50 to 60-years-old. She turned the heads of these Philistine men to where they were questioning if she was Isaac's wife. Here's where Isaac forgets God and trusts a lie to protect his skin. He's thinking these guys are after Rebekah, so he says, "She's my sister." Two things that give me pause here:
   a. Did he and his wife move into this town and leave most of their fighting servants behind, as well as Esau and Jacob, therefore fearing they could be overtaken by these Philistines and be harmed?
   b. Verse 8. It says, "when they'd been there a long time." Why didn't those men come for her then? (God's still protecting Isaac and Rebekah.) How long is a long time? It appears they were right in the middle of town. For the King, (not the same one in power when Abe did this same thing) from his castle window, saw them outside their tent actin' like a young, married couple getting excited with one another. All the information is a little sketchy, but now the "cats out of the bag" so to speak, and Ike is called before the King to answer for the lie. Verse 9. Basically, Ike feared for his life and confessed.
2. Verses 10 and 11. The King is ticked-off and chews on Ike for a while, then makes a "Decree." No Philistine man is to touch Rebekah. That puts an end to it, but the fear ended up bringing shame to Ike, I'm sure. God already told him, "I got your back, Ike." But the old sin nature jumped into high

gear and overcame his faith and bingo, trouble and later shame. Let that be a lesson for us. (Bet you'll fail.)

III. Like his father Abe, God blessed him nonetheless.

A. In the foreknowledge of God, He knew what Ike was going to do here even when he gave his word back in verses 2 to 5. So, time moves on, and Ike did some farming. Verse 12. "Sowed," this is the first time this word is used in the Bible. God blessed everything Ike touched; his wheat or barley (don't know which) a hundredfold, just like the parable of the sower in Matthew 13:8. What God intends to bless He will, and not because we're good guys. (If we are it's because He made us that.)

B. Verses 12 to 14. We see how much Ol' Ike is blessed by God. (What happened to the drought?) "Waxed Great" (Cool words, huh? KJ English.) He was probably richer than the King, which means he had an army of servants to care for all his wealth!

1. "Thou Shalt NOT Covet!" But we do, don't we? When somebody is doing better, we can get jealous. It's just in us that old sin nature is swelling up and ignoring the truth. Thanksgiving goes out the window, and these poor Philistines are only Born Once, so they don't get any help from God to stop and think things through honestly. Also, they, as we'll see, fear Isaac now. He just might conquer them and become their Ruler.

2. They think they'd hinder his growing stronger and maybe drive him out from them. Verse 15. The wells Isaac needed for his herds and flocks

the Philistines plugged. This is what started Ike to move.

Here's where we'll stop this week. Until the next study may God bless you and may you recognize this, that He is with you even in this troubled time.

Blessings, Mike

<u>Questions for Discussion</u>

1. We see two men of God struggle at times to have their faith match their circumstances. Read Romans 7:15–25. Key in on verse 18. Break it down into how many parts and what does that say about us as Born-Again children of God? Then go to verses 22 and 23. You see what's going on? Now think of fear stopping us from trusting God. The flesh seems to at times overpower us, whether it's lust or fear. Seems then our new spiritual life by the second birth (the inward man) depends on the Holy Spirit to stand in faith. Discuss this and see what ya come up with.

2. Isaac had strength in his servants to take from the Philistines, yet he didn't. Instead, he moved on. In Romans 12:17–21, we see this command that is really trusting the Lord to provide and deal with our enemies. God did that for Isaac. Can we apply this in our lives? What hinders us?

Finding a Place Where There's Room for Us

Let's see if we can get through chapter 26.

Let's pray.

Genesis 26:16–35 KJV

I. God's blessing to one man puts fear in another.

    A. Verse16. Abimelech saw not only a man of great herds but of Men in greater numbers than in his kingdom. Remember, in Genesis14:14, Abe had 318 "trained men," warriors from his own household. (Born of servants under Abe's authority.) I'm sure Ike had more. The King told Ike to leave the town of Gerar. The thing I see here is Isaac, like his father, was a man of Peace. He didn't fight back, though he could have, but moved on. He moved three times before the strife with the Philistines would stop.

        1. Verses 17 to 20. So those rascals, the Philistines, full of jealousy and fear, plugged up good wells that were in operation just to cause Ike to move on. But instead, Ike's men dug wells again, and one was a well that once dug started to flow and would not stop. It must have become a stream of "Spring Water." In the Greek Old Testament, spring water in this verse19 is called living water. Jesus used that as the ever-flowing, "ever-living"

Grace of God in John 4:10. But again, the local herdsmen started trouble with Ike's men, so Ike named the place Contention or Esek. He must not have moved too far but this was, he thought, far enough, only it wasn't. So, he moves again. They must have looked like a large tribe of Sioux Indians on the move with all their outfit, herds, and people. Probably a mile or two from the head of the herd to the back of the herd and Lord help those in the back! The dust had to be terrible.

2. Verse 21. So, they may not have moved far enough as I said earlier but tried to dig another well in the same general area. Sure enough, the Philistines got in their face about it, so Isaac called this well Hatred! or "Sitnah!" This, from what those who study Hebrew claim, is where we get the name Satan. Hatred is now serious, and so it's time, as the old trail bosses used to say, " Head 'um up! Move 'um Out!"

3. Verses 22 and 23. I'm looking on a map, and the topography from Gerar to the sea is pretty flat. I'm assuming that they were working their herd towards Beersheba which is a little south of east and the land rises. Somewhere it says, "they went up." They're talking land elevation. It doesn't say how far they moved from Gerar, but it was far enough, and they seemed to have a place to themselves and Peace! They called the place "Plenty Room!" or Rehoboth, for now the Lord has made room for us. Sounds like they had grazing for their herds all the way to Beersheba. Isaac recognized God's hand in this and was thankful. There seems to be a creek there that generally had water in it called Besor Brook. They were okay now. God said He'd bless them and He did.

II. Time with God and to worship Him.

  A. Beersheba is an important place in Genesis.

    1. Genesis 21:14-21. Beersheba is where Hagar went with her son Ishmael when they were run off. There the Lord met her and spoke to her concerning Ishmael.

    2. Abraham spent years here as well as this is where the first king mentioned of the Philistines met with Abe and made a peace treaty and where Abe planted a bunch of trees and called on the Lord. (Genesis 22:31–34) Abe was in Beersheba when God told him to offer up Isaac. Then he went back to Beersheba in Genesis 22:19. Apparently, the Philistines had a presence in that area as well as in Gerar. (Genesis 21:34)

    3. Isaac, we find here now, and God appears to him. Verse 24. He builds an altar to God and calls on the Lord. Verse 25. Then we see in verses 26 to 32, Isaac makes a peace treaty with perhaps the second King of the Philistines, as did Abe. Notice Abimelech recognizes God is with Ike, as also the other king did with Abe in Genesis 21:22. God was recognized by these Pagans and feared by how God protected and blessed Abe and then Isaac. Ike's servants were many. There were, I'm sure, trained servants in warfare as Abe had. That was a necessity in this pagan land. But as we've seen, fortunately for the Philistines, God made Ike a man of Peace. Seems he never had to go to battle.

    4. Also, we'll see God will meet here with Jacob. (Genesis 46:1–4)

  B. Beersheba means Well of Oaths which it has been

called ever since those days. Verse 33. These Oaths were made for the peace treaty and peace Isaac found in this land. He seems to be recognizing that the God of his father can, and should, be trusted. But as we'll see in the next study, Ike can be as Willful as me!

III. A child who won't follow the Lord can be a painful thing to parents.

A. Verse 34. Esau, the man of the hills, the man who seeks his passions, has been around these Pagans and takes two of their women. They were both Hittites from the hill country of that region. He could care less about the things of God or being separate from the Pagans of that country. He was not born-again. He did not obtain mercy from God but fulfilled the lust of the flesh. (Romans 9:10–13,16) As we'll see, Jacob wasn't much better but was still chosen of God.

   1. Verse 35. Isaac and Rebekah saw this, and love was there in them for their son. Seeing in the direction he was going did grieve them, as a Christian parent would be seeing the mercy of God was not on their son. They were praying God would intervene.

B. Here in these two studies, man who wasn't perfect but sanctified failed to trust God. Yet, God did not fail him. I believe we can remember this for us and our walk with Him.

Blessings, Mike

Questions for Discussion

1. Part of God's omniscience is foreknowledge, so God knows beforehand the times we will fail. Looking at Abe and Ike, we saw God allowed this. He could have prevented it, but He didn't. It appears at the end of these episodes; things turned out exactly where God wanted them to be, and the relationship was restored. How about in your life?

The Motives of this Family are Disturbing Willfulness, Deception, and Hate

Well, in this chapter, Isaac's family is getting complicated. Seems willful sin will do that. Anger and fear take control of this family. Jacob is the main character for many chapters. Some commentators seem to think he was spiritually right and saw Esau could care less about the things of God, as well as he knew the Promises God made were through him. But he took matters into his own hands to help fulfill God's will. I'm not sure that is the right view of Jake. I think he's a selfish man who wants it all for himself. Whatever is the motive of man, good intended or NOT, God is directing this according to His Will. So, let's take a look. (Isaiah 14:24)

Let's pray.

Genesis 27:1–30 KJV

I. Isaac is ignoring God's Will and seeking his own and is determined Esau will be Blessed.

A. Looking back to Genesis 25:22–23, God told Rebekah that Jacob would receive the Blessing. In Romans 9: 10–13, this matter is more clarified as to what God said. It's hard to believe Isaac doesn't know this, as well as how care-less Esau is toward the things of God. He's also married two Hittite women, and was careless of his Birthright, selling it to Jacob for a bowl of beans. Yet here in verse 1, Ike intends to Bless this heathen Esau anyway. We see in Genesis 25:28, because of Esau's physical wild skills and bravery, Ike favors him over Jacob. I'm sure this hurts Jacob who seems to be the responsible one over the family business of the herds and flocks. Later we'll also see this favoritism in Jacob concerning his children. But we need to be careful about us getting too hard on these guys without seeing perhaps some of our own willfulness in our own lives. Know that behind what we read here, God is directing this story to play out the way He intends.

1. Verses 1 to 4. Ike thinks he's going to die soon so he's made up his mind he's gonna give Esau the Blessing. Here we need to understand what a Blessing is at this time. This is not a father to son in the family line but is Prophetic. This is passing the "Seed of the Woman" down to the next generation as the "Seed Transporter," as well as passing down the Line of the Nation which will be Israel. Ike is going to give it to the son that could care less of the importance of this, but still wanted the Blessing for self-gain. (Esau thinking of the family wealth as I'm thinking Jacob also wanted. He'd already stolen the double portion of the family inheritance from his older twin brother.) But nonetheless, this Blessing needs to be understood as a God-given transfer of what was vital for ALL people on Earth. Like the example of Noah blessing Shem, "Blessed be the Lord God of Shem." That's God speaking through man. Here Ike thinks he's gonna pull a fast one on God, but little does he know God has that figured out already and continues His-Story on schedule!

B. Verses 5 to 17. God lines this conversation up so Rebekah could overhear this foolishness of her husband.

1. And in verse 9, like the bold woman she was, she set to work to get the Blessing to the son whom God said was to have it. (Having a husband with cataracts on his eyes was handy to deceive him.) So, she rounds up Jake and tells him what to do. Verses 9 and 10.
2. Jake doesn't think it'll work (verse 12), but Rebekah knows what God said and trusts God. Or maybe she's doing this because Jake is her baby like Esau is Ike's favorite. She's going to get Jake there first to dishonestly receive the Blessing. Whatever the motive, God is going to have Jacob receive the Blessing. So, Rebekah tells Jake to follow her instructions.

B. Verses 14 to 17. They follow through. Jake gets the two kid goats. Ma goes to Esau's tent to find some of his clothes for Jake to wear and has some skins from a kid goat to put on his arm and neck. Then she cooks up the meat and gives it to Jake to take to his father. So, here he goes.

1. God doesn't condone lying; the Ten Commandments "Thou shall not bear false witness." (Don't Lie.) But we see later in Egypt the midwives saving baby boys. (Exodus 1:15–20) Then Rahab in Joshua 2:1–6. How all this works out in God's thinking, I don't know, but in the foreknowledge of God, this was the way it was to go down. God could have killed Esau but had plans for him to father a wicked nation of Edom.

II. The deception and the giving of the Blessing to Jacob.
   A. To start out, God, remember, is sovereign. This situation didn't get out of His control. He could have caused it to go down a different way, but this willfulness, of Isaac, the care-lessness of Esau, and the outright lying of Jacob is how it's going to be to accomplish. God's will is to be done, and Jacob will receive the Blessing.

1. Verses18 to 20. Here Jake lies twice. Ike knows his two son's voices and questions if it's not really Jake. Verses 20 to 22 tell Jacob to come, and Isaac feels if it's Esau. The goat hair tricks him, or maybe he's just going along with it cause he knows who's supposed to really receive the Blessing and knows what's going on. (I don't know, just speculating possibilities.) In verse 23, Ike said, "yet, that's my hairy son, Esau." So, he blesses Jake. What Blessing this was I don't know cause later in verses 28 and 29 the Covenant Blessing is given.

2. Verse 24. Again, Ike questions if this is really Esau? Again, Jake lies. It says in verse 25, "bring the food here along with some wine," and he ate and drank. Then again, Isaac said, "Come here close to me; kiss me." Verse 26. When Jake did, he smelled Esau and again Ike was tricked into thinkin' Jake was Esau. Verse 27.

3. So, in this whole thing that went on, Jacob lies three times! God gave Isaac belief in his senses of feel, taste, and smell over his sense of hearing and concluded this was Esau.

   B. The Blessing is given verses 28 and 29 and is three-fold.

1. God will make Jacob very fruitful as we'll see.

2. "Let people serve you, Nations bow down before you." I personally think this is God proclaiming the "Seed of the Woman" is through Jacob. (Philippians 2:10–11)
3. Here is the trick on Isaac. He, thinkin' Jake is Esau says, "you will be over that son your mother likes so much!" But as God said, "The Older WILL serve the Younger." It turned out exactly how God intended it to be.
4. Then goes on to say what God told Abraham in Genesis 12:3 concerning what would happen to those with how they treat Jacob.

C. Verse 30. With the Blessing now given to whom God intended to give it to done, Jacob departs. The deed is done! This is a Covenant Blessing meaning irrevocable (can't change). Shortly thereafter, Esau comes in. It's all done the way God said it would be. Why this way with deception and outright lying, I don't know. The willfulness of Isaac and the care-lessness of Esau seemed to override the sin of Rebekah and Jacob. I'll trust God to deal with the reasoning behind all this.

1. One thing we need to remember about Ol' Isaac is back in chapter 22. He, at that time, was stronger than his father, Abraham. Ike could have stopped the whole thing of himself going to the altar to be killed as a burnt offering. But he didn't. He wasn't being willful then. Like Jesus said, "No one takes my life, but I freely give it." So did Isaac. Later he had some "short, dumb spells." We see in between there were times he did also trust God. (Sounds like me!)
2. Let that be looked at as what should be recognized within ourselves. We may trust Him one time and go through the "Fire" so to speak, then

fail the next time. These people are human like we are. God in the person of Jesus is the only one who didn't fail. So, by Grace, we stand. Thank you, Lord! Amen.

We're going to be travelin' up to "Me Island" in MN. It may be a couple weeks before I get any more studied out.

May God keep ya till then! Mike

Question for Discussion

1. Think over section II. C. 1. and 2. So many studies focus on what we should or shouldn't do and use these as examples. But my thought on this is the best we can really do is recognize we will fail and recognize 1 Corinthians 10:12 and 1 John 1:9. Knowing how much we must depend on God to stand. Remember, James 4:6. We, with the new spiritual life given us, desire righteousness. (Romans 7:22) That's the part that's eternal, and one day we will be free from what is explained in Romans 7:23. So, we look to that time. (Romans 8:18) That focus makes us fail less.

God Uses the Wrath of Esau to Send Jake to Get a Shemite Bride or Two

Howdy, folks. We're back home on "Me Island." Long time in the saddle from AZ, about 2,000 miles. Thank the Lord we're safely Home! Let's see if we can finish chapter 27.

Let's pray.

Genesis 27:31–46 KJV

I. An unpleasant surprise for Esau.

A. Verses 31 to 33. Isaac's pulling a fast one on God. He comes to the reality it didn't work, as well as Ike realizes he was treading on thin ice! What I'm saying is:

1. At first, Ike's wondering what's going on?
2. Then it hits him like a thunderbolt he's been tricked into Blessing the one who was to get the Blessing in the first place, Jacob that rascal! The one that woman of mine Loves!
3. The Hebrew Bible scholars claim in verse 33, "trembled very exceedingly" is not quite good enough to explain how strong the mixed emotions were going on inside Isaac. First, a mixture of anger and disappointment, then fear of God that Rebekah and Jacob had to deceive him into doing God's purpose that he was in rebellion of. That realization caused fear! Then shame for all

that God taught him through his father Abraham, he ignored so as not to pass on the Blessing to whom God intended to carry the "Seed of the Woman" and instead satisfy his carnal desires based on pride NOT thanksgiving! He realized he could have found himself in God's wrath!

4. So, he concluded in verse 33, "and he Shall be Blessed!" meaning Jacob the one God had chosen, the one God loved shall be ordained as carrying God's promises. In him shall the Nation of Israel come, and the savior of the world with the protection of God.

B. Verses 34 to 38. Esau is shocked! What's going on! In verse 35, Isaac answers, "Your brother has played me the fool. I gave the Blessing to Jacob," and as in verse 33, "and he shall be Blessed!" Irrevocable! What's done is done! Jacob is the Trickster! He's named well! He now, by taking Esau's birthright, gets a double portion of the family wealth. "He is ruler of all our father has: livestock, riches, and servants, as well as God's protection and fruitfulness. I have nothing." (Well Esau, you could care less for things of God before, you don't like responsibility, why is this a big a deal now to ya? My thoughts, but how often in the past have I too, been similar to Esau?) No Esau, you'll have much. God is going to raise up the wicked nation of Edom through you, but you don't know that yet. The fact is, this life is ALL you'll have, Esau. You'd do well to read what God said about you in Malachi 1:2–4. God has chosen to love that rascal Jacob and REJECT you! Jacob doesn't deserve it either but I, God of ALL, hath Chosen him nonetheless. Sin made life tuff, and then ya die. (The second death, Esau and there you'll face a terror beyond anything anyone has faced in this LIFE!)

1. We need to keep in mind Romans 9:11 in all this. This applies to all of us too. Grace is absolutely the choice of the giver, not the receiver. (If we had a choice, we'd run from God not to Him, for born once, we are slaves to sin, and we have no choice.)
2. Verses 37 and 38. Ike compounds the shock stating, "By the power God's given me, I have made Jacob ruler over you and all my servants." The question Ike states in this verse is not, "what shall I do for you?" but a statement, "what God has pre-determined cannot be changed." This Man of the World who feared nothing is brought to weeping like a baby. Begging yet to no avail. What's done is done!

II. What he gets is a struggle to survive!

A. Verses 39 to 40. The nation of Edom that Esau will start will be on dry land, not well-watered. Violence will be the rule.

1. The King James Bible goofed up here in verse 39 where it says, "be the Fatness of the earth." Should be AWAY from the fatness of the Earth. The area that he settles in is a poor, hot, rugged region.
2. In verse 40, the King James Bible should not have used dominion but shake away the bonds Jacob has over you. Then the yoke shall be loosed from you.
   a. One thing I don't understand is while this says Jacob will receive what Isaac has, yet we'll see he makes his fortune, with God's blessing, from working for his father-in-law. I don't read where he ever received from Ike what was to be his. Perhaps it's assumed after he and Esau

buried their father. Perhaps it was given him. We will find later that Esau is as happy as a fat cat and doesn't need anything from Jacob. So, the Blessing of "fruitfulness" will be noticed in all Jacob does.

III. Now God uses Esau's anger to send Jacob to Laban to start the family that will become Israel.

A. Verse 41. This is the same anger that fired up Cain to kill Abel. If you remember in the 1 John 3:12–15 study, the completion of or end of hate or anger is to kill who you hate, so that potential is in us. What keeps one from the completion of hate, or lets us fall to that depth of depravity, is God.

B. Verses 42 to 45. God gets word to Rebekah, and she calls Jake to her and tells him to get out of Dodge! Put on the big skedaddle! Now obviously their camp is big: many tents. Esau is going to wait till Isaac dies, but they don't want Esau to find Jacob. That may just cause him to forget to wait till his dad dies. Jacob needs to get going. Verse 43. As we'll see, Jake will be staying with Uncle Laban a lot longer than a few days. Verse 44.

1. Verse 45. Rebekah says, "Why should I be deprived of two sons?" Apparently, in the unwritten laws of that time, if one kills someone in their family, an Elder relative must take vengeance, meaning kill Esau. Therefore, Rebekah's thought is I'd have no sons!

2. So, in verse 46, we end with Rebekah going to Isaac and requesting Ike to tell Jake to go to her family and take a bride, not one of these Canaanite girls. (This is what God intends for the twelve tribes of Israel; to start as purebred Shemites.

That is if Leah, and Rachel's handmaids, were Shemites too for some of his sons will be from them.)

Conclusion: Sin does confuse things, and man does confuse things more than should be, but God will use that to get the end results He intends. Therefore, showing us time and again what Satan thinks he'll destroy, God will use for His purpose. Romans 15:4 comes to mind. That word Hope could be replaced with the word Confidence. Confidence in the fact God is able, we can trust Him with our lives.

Well until next time. Blessings to ya, Mike

Questions for Discussion

1. So, was Isaac in rebellion of God? (1 Samuel 15:23) Sounds like rebellion and stubbornness go together.
2. Remember Deuteronomy 9:4–6? With all that Isaac has seen of the Lord, it's strange that he'd go against God. But it seems he did. Yet God was merciful to him, not Saul whose throne he took away and gave to David. Can you see God's sovereign choice with these examples? Jacob have I loved, but Esau have I hated.

Concerning Isaac, 2 Timothy 2:25; God Accomplishes His Purpose in His People, as well as Those of This World

Mornin' folks. Some of you who write to me from time to time it seems God is leading you with a clear vision of what He wants you to do for His Kingdom. We're praying for you and praising Him for you. This has been a very helpful study for me and hope it has for those of you who have time to study this with me. I know in this time that you and I live, it seems there are so many things that get in the way, yet God is faithful. For many of you, your focus is on another study and can't spend the time where we are in this study. I'm sending these studies with that understanding. Some have requested these studies, while others I just send it to thinking you may or may not have a need for such a study, or may or may not be interested, which is fine with me.

Let's pray.

Genesis 28:1–9 KJV

I. Isaac's turnabout or repentance.

A. As we saw in Genesis 27:46, Isaac's helpmate God uses to influence him. We saw in Genesis 27:33 that God put fear in Ike, and so Ike is ready to listen now and be directed. God was as He always is, in control and directing this exactly as He intended. Yes, Ike was rebellious.

God allowed his old sin nature to carry him away in rebellion for a season and now that things are shaken up, God steps in and grants Isaac repentance.

1. Look at 2 Timothy 2:25. Now the whole thought begins in verse 24 and ends in 26, but the important part is verse 25 where we first see God telling through someone who speaks truth to one who opposes themselves. (That's a good way to say it for that's what's really going on.) And peradventure (meaning perhaps) God WILL GIVE repentance to or enable the one in rebellion to repent. I know we don't see repenting that way. We FEEL like it's us that have made the decision, but if we are Born-Again Children of God, the NEW nature or heart God gives us does, and will, always desire to do God's will. (See Romans 7:15,18,22 then 25.) By all means, read it all, but focus on those verses. Verse 22 is the New Spiritual Life that will never die and delights in the Law of God. (The word law means a force of influence and in this case, righteousness.) This spiritual life His Children will always delight in. BUT! We see, in verse 23, the old sin nature (members or flesh) is a Bully and stronger than our new Nature, minus God, the Holy Spirit, and will take us captive, and as verse 15 says, "I do the things I hate."
   a. The question we can't understand is then why does He hold me accountable if we only want to please him but get bullied into doing sin?
   b. Why does He, the Holy Spirit, let us fall?
2. There are many verses that show we are accountable and are commanded to do things that will make us stand in His power. (See Ephesians 5:18–21 and 1 Corinthians 10:13, 11:28–32.) Yet

what we see in all this it's not us by ourselves who are able to do them, but God who Enables us to. For instance, 1 Corinthians 7:7. That gift is God protecting one saint where a particular sin can't take root. Therefore, he doesn't have trouble with temptation in that area of his life, whereas some other brothers have temptation. That's God's doing. The paradox is, like between for instance, Romans 6:12 and 7:15–25, that while both are facts and true (for they're both in His word), so often we just ignore Romans 7:15–25 and stay in Romans 6:12 and preach you must choose to obey. While some of you seem not to have a problem; ignoring verses 22 and 23 and not acknowledging it's God who is enabling you to stand against sin. They're preachin' this minus 7:15–25. Some, on the other hand, are not able to stand and fall not knowing their hope is in the forgiveness of God and to humbly confess their failings (1 John 1:9) and ask Him for the strength to stand. Both need to be taught even when Theologians don't understand (for instance, God is one, yet the Trinity). We must have Faith in what God says even when we don't see the how's or the wherefores. God will sort this out for us by and by.

3. I said all that to recognize that it's God who worketh in us (Philippians 2:13) and enables us to overcome the Old Sin Nature and repent as here with Isaac. God never lets something happen that he does not intend to happen. He has a purpose for all that happens and, in this case, Isaac's rebellion, and repentance. This doesn't let Ol' Ike off the hook for his rebellion. Yet he is forgiven by his repentance that God enabled him to do. (Sure seems odd to interesting, that by God

we are made able to repent, but yet, like when He holds us accountable when we sin, by our old sin nature taking us captive to do the things we hate. Then He stops that dead thing that takes us captive and releases us to be able to turn back to Him and receive forgiveness; grace. We don't deserve any credit, yet He gives us credit. I'm betting there's some out there reading this that don't understand this, and even disagree with the summary of this that I'm presenting. It would not hurt my feelings to hear from you. I won't argue but will present Scripture. Nonetheless, Isaac is now commanding and giving the whole Blessing to Jacob without deception, nor without pride and lust controlling him. His inward man is free to do the will of God. I'm sure there's much relief to Ike's inner-being for he's now right with God. The short, dumb spell that was cast on him is over. Now we will watch God work with Jacob.

B. Verses 1,2,5. The Command. You, Jake, go to our Shemite family up in Padan-aram and take a cousin of yours for a wife. God wants purebred offspring to build His promised nation. You get goin' right now! Ike's thinkin', "Thanks to me, we've fooled around too long!"

C. Verses 3,4. The Blessings are repeated by Isaac without being deceived.

1. God will make thee fruitful.
2. Make thee a multitude of people.
3. The Blessing of his grandfather that is all the land God gave Abe, God will give Jacob and his children. (Of course, in this nation will be the "Seed of the Woman.")

Jake takes off. Is he alone or with some of his servants? It doesn't say one way or another. The focus is now just on Jacob. Verse 5.

II. Esau sees this time the Blessing was given with his father truly meaning it.

A. Verses 6 to 9. Realizing he has not pleased his parents with his could care less attitude, Esau thinks well, Uncle Ismael's clan are 1/2 or 1/4 Shemites. Maybe I'll go get me one of their daughters, which he does. See in verse 9, the girl's name is Mahalath, who is probably Abraham's great-granddaughter. This is an interesting story God has made for this part or leg of the trail of the "Seed of the Woman." God lets Satan time and again attempt to destroy the Seed, but he never can. Therefore, our Hope is secure knowing what has been done; we can be confident we will be with Him at His appointed time for each of us.

This is enough for now. We'll be lookin' at Jacob's ladder next study and Jake's response.

Have a Blessed week! Mike

Question for Discussion

1. I. A. 1., 2., and 3. You need to seriously look at this. Study it out. A good verse to think of as you think through this again is Proverbs 3:6, particularly the word All. How extensive is that? Does ALL really mean all?

God is Leading

Mornin' folks. We got rain, wind, and chilly temps today. But that's ok, we have plenty of wood and got this study to do. In the Bible study over on the Reservation last week, in Philippians 3:1, rejoicing in the Lord leads to safety or security. Why? Because joy is "remembering the value of something you possess." We have Jesus, our Lord, and God the Father's love when we remember this. We are safe in Him; therefore we are secure in Him against the wiles of the Devil. We can stand God's armor on. We're safe. Thought that was a good reminder. Likewise, when we forget we get caught up in the world and for a season are not safe, have no peace, and struggle. As we look at this study, we see God on every page leading Jacob, which should give us confidence in God. Jeremiah 10:23; Proverbs 20:24 and16:9, our lives are not a crapshoot. God's purpose will prevail in us, safe for us. (Romans 8:1)

Let's pray.

Genesis 28:10–22 KJV

I. Jacob makes camp in a place where God meets him.

A. This place is the second place God met Abraham in Canaan. (Genesis 12:8; 13:3) Here Jacob camped. It appears he's traveling alone, probably with a donkey and a small outfit (I'm guessing), no tent. With good weather, he camps under the stars. Nonetheless, Jake, like a good

Korean uses a rock for a pillow. (That'd give me a head-ache.) Verses 10 and 11. This is north of Jerusalem about 70 miles from Beersheba, so this must be the second or third night.

B. He dreamed, and what he saw was a ladder; that its foot was on the earth and it rested on Heaven. Verse 12. And Angels were going and coming on this ladder. The idea I believe, and others think too, is about the inter-relationship between Heaven and Earth. There's intense interest in the goings on down here.

1. If you could pull back the veil between the natural world and the Spiritual, and see the spiritual forces that are really involved with directing the physical world, you'd be amazed! Nonetheless, that's what Jake saw in the dream.
2. Verse 13. God is looking down from Heaven and introduces Himself to Jake. "I Am the Lord God of Abraham, and the God of Isaac." He then reasserts the promises He stated to Jake's grandpa and father, that also Isaac had Blessed Jacob with earlier.
   a. The land you're sleepin' on I give to you and your children.
   b. You'll have so many kids, grandkids, and so on beyond your imagination.
   c. And then the important one; that without this, the others wouldn't matter, the "Seed of the Woman." Christ will come through you who will save the world from their sin.
   d. I'll protect you. I am your strong and mighty Fortress!
   e. You're about to leave this place, but I'll bring you back here, don't you worry!

    f. I won't leave you ever, and then I'll bring you home! (When I accomplish what I intend to accomplish in you.)

  3. Back to that ladder. Jesus mentioned He was that ladder. (John 1:51) Here He calls Himself, "The Son of Man." It was His favorite title. He called Himself that 80 times in the Gospels. This refers to His mission. God becomes Man to make man right with God. God becomes Man. In John.14:6 where He said, "I Am the Way." (I am that ladder.)

II. Time to get up.

A. Verse 16. He realized this was not just a mindless, wondering dream, but God showing Jacob His purpose for him and that this was a special place. He didn't realize.

  1. Verse 17. Fear took hold of him. I'm sure Jake understood the doctrine of God's omnipresence. God in all places at the same time. He is Spirit. Yet the realization God was here visiting him for an important revelation humbled Jake; he was in the presence of God!

  2. I'm thinkin' Jacob was instructed in the fall of Adam as well as the flood, tower of Babel, and Isaac's birth, along with the promise of Genesis 3:15. But God now has shown Himself to Jacob at this place, and we'll see this isn't the last time either.

III. Jacob worships God here as well as makes an oath.

A. Verses 18 and 19. He takes the stone he rested his head upon, stood it upright to make an altar (probably wasn't too tall), and poured oil on it (showing he must have had a camp outfit with him). This was how he learned to consecrate a special place of worship. Oil was precious. Then the place was called Luz, but now Jake renames it "House of God" – Bethel. It seems God liked that name for somehow this place was from then on changed to Bethel.

B. Verse 21 and 22. A vow was given. At first, this sounds like Jacob is saying IF you perform all that you said in that dream, THEN I will worship you. (I was seeing this that way too.) But! it's the Oath or Vow; Jake was realizing, that God has promised what He did and Jacob trusted His Word. We could use the word SINCE instead of IF. The same thought has confused people in the New Testament. In several places, the word "IF" was used where one could take it as works will bring salvation (Romans 8:11), "but IF the Spirit . . ." IF is alright if you understand if is used like since. (Colossians 1:23) "If you continue . . ." It's like if you stop and stumble you lose, whereas since you are Born-Again and sealed with the Holy Spirit, you can't. (Philippians1:6; Ephesians 1:13–14) We have to ALWAYS remember we are saved by Grace not works in any way.

1. So, SINCE you, God, have promised me these things; You are my God! Therefore, all that You give me I will give a tenth back to You, my Lord, my God. Just like Grandpa Abraham did to the Priest of the most-High God, Melchizedek. (This then shows us they understood what then wasn't written down. Recognizing a "Sovereign," then we giving back is proper worship.

2. We see here God is teaching the "Trickster," "The Heal Grabber." God is with him. We'll see some struggles with Jacob's faith, but in the end,

his Faith will be recognized in Hebrews 11 and again, Romans 15:4. This true story should build our confidence in Him, who is able!

Until next time. God is WITH you!

Blessings, Mike

Question for Discussion

1. Read Matthew 25:31–40. Is this what He's talking about? Worship?

Jacob Meets his Uncle Laban and Seeks a Bride; Gets Two plus Two Concubines!

Mornin' folks. Had to preach last Sunday, so didn't get this study out. Preachin' this Sunday too but got it pretty well figured out. Will see if I can finish this by this Friday. (It's now Monday that I'm finishing it, so I didn't.)

Let's pray.

Genesis 29:1–30 KJV

I. By the providence of God Jake is directed to his mother's family.

   A. The end of his journey is at hand. He meets herdsmen from Haran. Verses 1 to 4.

   B. He asks where they're from and by the providence of God they are from Haran. Jake wants to know if they know his uncle Laban. Of course, they do because God has led him to here to meet the love of his life, Laban's daughter. Verses 5 and 6.

      1. Now Jake suggests they water their sheep and get to grazing them. Probably wants to be alone with Rachel and introduce himself as her cousin. But

it was too late anyway for she's already too near. Verses 7 to 9.

2. Verses 10 to 12. We see Jake then takes matters into his own hands and moves the rock off the well. Jewish commentators say the reason the shepherds were waiting was the rock was heavy. They were amazed that this one could move it easily. (So was I. I figure Jake as kind of a creampuff.) Anyway, he waters Rachel's sheep, and not till after that, does he introduce himself to this fair young lady and kisses her with the customary kiss to greet one's relative. He is so amazed that God brought him directly to his mother's family. Rachel quickly gets excited and runs to tell her father.

   a. Now how old is Jake? There seem to be two lines of figures of thinking here. The common one starts when Jake met the Pharaoh at age 130 (Genesis 47:9), and then you back up from there to places where age and or years were mentioned, and it seems he was 77-years-old at this time. However, there's another study that claims he was in his mid-60's. But none-theless Jake was past when most men take a wife and, of course, this was God's timing. Esau was married and had many kids by now. Seems he was 40 when he took two Hittite women.

II. The meeting with Jake's Uncle Laban.

A. Here Jake is right where God intended (as always is the case). This is a joyous time. Jacob realizes God is with him as God said He would be in Bethel. While he waits, he's watching the sheep for his future wife.

1. Verses 13 and 14. Laban is told about Jacob. Excited to see family, he runs to meet Jake. Jake tells of the goings on in the family and proclaims that you are my blood family, what is mine is yours, welcome! So, Jake stays a while.

III. Jacob makes a deal with Uncle Laban to marry Rachel but ends up with Leah too.

A. Verse 15. It seems Laban saw that Jake was a "Top Hand" and wanted him to stay working for him. So, he asks Jake to name his price. Remember God said he'd bless Jake and be with him. Laban recognizes Jake is profitable to keep him serving him. Laban isn't a believer in the "Most-High God" as Jake is, but sees his worth.

1. Verses 16 to 19. Jake is willing to work seven years for the love of his life, Rachel. Leah didn't seem to excite him. "Tender-Eyed;" the commentators don't agree in their thoughts about the meaning. Some think she had something wrong with her eyes, others that she hurt the eyes of those seeing her, and still others believe it meant she had compassion. Regardless, Jake wasn't interested in her and wanted the younger Rachel. Laban agrees.

2. Uncle Laban pulls a fast one on the "Trickster." Jake's seven years flew by, and he was ready for payday and asks for his wife. Verses 20 and 21. So Uncle Laban throws a big party and there's much wine. The bride is probably "veiled," and it's dark by the time he is to take his bride to bed, and not knowing, he slept with Leah!

3. Verse 24. Laban was a wealthy herdsman, and as was the custom of those times and place, he gave Zilpah to serve Leah.

B. Verse 25. Upon waking Jake sees the face of the wrong daughter. Probably with anger, he seeks Laban and demands an answer! Laban gives him one in Verse 26; the first-born has to be married before the younger. You want Rachel; you be with Leah for a week. That will, to Leah, guarantee she is Jacob's wife and not bring shame on the household of Laban. Then and only then will Laban give Rachel to Jake. Verse 27. But Jake must give his word he'll work seven more years also.

C. Jake agrees, waits a week and then is given Rachel. As customary, Laban gives Rachel a handmaid, named Bilhah. Verses 28 and 29.

1. We end this study with Verse 30. Rachel, the love of his life, is now his.
2. Now God has Jacob all set to not only start his family but has the women that will be used to make the twelve tribes of Israel. The old trickster, Jacob, was tricked himself through God using Laban.

This will be the last of the "PURE Blood" Shemites. Jake's sons will take wives from Hamites, as we'll see. We need to remember God is working this all out ACCORDING to the counsel of His own Will. As He does in ALL our lives.

God's Blessings to ya, Mike

Wives and Sons of Jacob; Things aren't the Happiest

Howdy, folks. We're back from North Carolina and my aunt's funeral. So, let's see what we can get studied. Jake's a married man now times four, and what a mess. But! God's got His reasons and has this lined out to make twelve tribes of Israel from these twelve sons of Jacob.

Let's pray.

Genesis 29:31–35, 30:1–24 KJV

I. Poor Leah!

A. Verses 31-35. This isn't really Jake's fault. He loved Rachel but got tricked by his new father-in-law. (Still what goes around comes around, and he's the Ol' heal grabber, trickster remember.) You can see the pain in Leah and the need to be loved by her OWN husband. Think if you were in Leah's shoes. Her husband has sex with her, but she knows he's thinkin' of Rachel. She goes through the pain and suffering of having a child and each time she gives hope to God that her husband will now love her; yet each time it's the same. Poor Leah!

1. Jake, on the other hand, as we'll see, isn't recognizing God's hand in all this and can't love unconditionally. His attitude is selfish. He singles out Rachel and her kids to love before all the

others. It leads the boys to become a bitter, mean bunch.

2. He's a man and I'm sure lusts like any other man, so he's not going to say no when offered the sexual services that his two wives offer him with themselves and their "handmaids." I'm sure he, in some way, recognizes these kids as his and, therefore, has some feelings of love towards them but apparently openly acknowledges Rachel and her kids first. This is gonna really mess the family up as we will see.

3. So, Leah has Reuben whose name means, "look a son," Simon whose name means "hearing," as in God heard my prayers, Levi meaning "attachment" as in now my husband will recognize us as one, and then Judah whose name means "praise," as she's now praising God. Verse 31. The Lord saw Leah was hated, so He closed up Rachel's womb and opened Leah's, yet Jake couldn't see his own wrong thinkin'. Verse 35. Leah is praising God. Seems she's a woman of faith while we'll see a few things about Rachel that will give us some pause as to her faith in the One, True God.

II. Competition between the wives is fierce!

A. Chapter 30, verses 1 and 2. We see Rachel is hurt and jealous of Leah. Not knowing the why of things. Verse 31. The argument gets heated, and Jake points to the fact it's not in his control! Which is right. Here the providential opening of the womb is God's choice. Ephesians.1:11 – "who worketh ALL things after the counsel of HIS OWN WILL." So now Rachel thinks she'll solve her problem by . . .

1. Verse 3. This may be the tradition of the time. She gives Bilhah to Jake for bearing children in her stead. "Upon my knee" means she will acknowledge them as hers.

B. Verses 4 to 8. We see it was in God's plan for Bilhah had Dan, whose name means "justice." Now Rachel feels vindicated by God. Then Jake goes into Bilhah again, and she has another son and Rachel names this one Naphtali which means "wrestling." Verse 8 comments, "for I have prevailed" (some pride appearing in Rachel).

C. Now it's Leah's turn to be jealous. Verse 9. Bearing kids seems to be the main focus between the two sisters. Seems Jake was a very virile man and was having sex regularly with Leah, but she wasn't getting pregnant, so she followed Rachel's example and gave Zilpah to Jake. He seemed to enjoy Zilpah and continued spending time with her for she had not just one, but two boys. Leah named the first Gad, which means "luck" in pagan but is also used for good fortune. (We hope she sees God's blessing, not the pagan thinking.) Verses 12 and 13. The next son she named Asher, meaning "happy." Women will see her as blessed. We like others to respect us, and back then if not now also, a woman with many sons was envied. Leah liked that.

1. Now they have eight boys. Eight tribes of Israel. Still, four more to come.

III. Them mandrakes.

A. Verses 14 and 15. As we see, there were plants God made that are helpful for various ailments. This one seemed to help women's wombs to become more open so as to become pregnant. Leah's oldest boy found them in someone's wheat field and brought them to his mother. But Rachel saw them and desired them for herself. So, let's make a deal. Rachel said bring Jake to yourself tonight and give me the mandrakes. They agreed. Leah enticed Jake to come to her bed (which probably wasn't hard), and she got pregnant. Verse 16. Leah comes right out and says to Jake of the deal with Rachel over the mandrakes, so he went into her.

1. Verses 17 to 21. God again opened Leah's womb, and out came Issachar! Which is the "reward" for the GOOD trade with Rachel. But again, all this was God's plan, and He intended her to have another still and by golly, if Ol' Jake didn't keep seeing her and *Boom!* another came into this world! She named him Zebulun (we'll call him Zeb). The meaning of Zeb's name is "dwelling." Her thought was MY husband is now dwelling with me! It seems he comes to her again. She becomes pregnant, but this time it's a girl she named Dinah. (There's gonna be a problem later in chapter 34 over Dinah.)

2. So now God has ten Tribes of Israel accounted for! Two more to go!

B. Now is God's appointed time for Rachel to give Jacob sons. Verses 22 to 24. "God remembered Rachel." (Not that He forgets. Just like with Noah in the Ark. Genesis 8:1 it says, "He remembered," but we know He's not like us who forget, is He?) God looks on her with loving favor is the idea.

1. The first one she calls Joseph, which has one of two meanings, either, "may the Lord add" or "He has taken away." (He has taken away my reproach.) Joseph will have an important part in the

making and protecting of this family who will become a Nation but will be loved, some much more than the others. They will hate him enough to want him dead! The last is Benjamin and Rachel will die bearing him. (Genesis 35:18)

So, there is the start of the Nation God promised Abraham. The thing we can see (really one of the things we can see) is God will use man's sinful nature to accomplish His purpose. "After the Counsel of His own Will." His chosen nation will be made-up of purebred Rascals! Sinners just like us. The verse in Romans 9:15 holds true in all of His-Story. We're all a bunch of lusting, prideful rascals! Check out again Deuteronomy 9:4–6; Romans 3:11–20, and 1 Corinthians 1:29.

Blessings, Mike

Question for Discussion

1. These men, Abe all the way to Benjamin, were "men of the land." They were rough, not afraid of dirt, used to killing to eat and to defend or even take from someone else. They could travel in extreme heat or heavy rain and cold, go without a meal or three, and keep going. They were rough talking, rugged men. Like Mongol herdsmen or cowboys back a 150-years ago. In my thinkin' (man to man) they were to be respected. Of course, they were sinners, rascals apart from God's grace. I think many Christians don't picture them as they really were because we live in such an artificial society.

God Keeps His Word. Jacob will be Cared For, even with Crafty Uncle Laban

Howdy, folks. Hope this finds ya all hopeful (confident in Him), and joyful (remembering the value of what you possess). Well, let's see what God reveals to us this week.

Let's pray.

Genesis 30:25–43 KJV

A. Verses 25 and 26. Now Rachel has finally given him a son, Joseph. Jake worked out his agreement of 14 years. He asks Laban to let him go home.

B. Verses 27 and 28. Laban knows his flocks have grown great because of God's favor on Jacob and wants Jake to stay and basically says, "Name your wage, I'll pay it to keep you."

   1. Now Ol' Uncle Laban has proven he's like the street "one way" (to himself) and can't be trusted which we'll see in Genesis 31:7.

C. Verses 29, 30, and 31. Jake reminds Laban he had a small flock before and has much now because of God's blessing on Jake, but now I need to get going on a flock of my own and care for my family. Laban acknowledges this and again says name your price.

II. My wage will not cost you anything that you have now but will be by the Lord.

A. As I study Ol' Jake again, I'm beginning at this go-round to recognize he had more faith and understanding than I had in the past saw. All that he has accomplished tending Laban's flock; the growing is God blessing his work.

B. Verses 32 to 34. The King James Bible used different meanings for words back then and is confusing. They didn't have cattle, only sheep and goats. The word, cattle, refers to the idea of "pushing out a member of the flock to graze;" to separate that bunch from the rest. So, Jake says separate all.

1. Speckled and spotted SHEEP.
2. Every black LAMB.
3. Every speckled and spotted GOAT.
4. And SUCH will pay my wage.

C. You can search my flock and see if I'm cheating you or stealing from you. Verse 34. Laban agrees.

1. The idea is to search all the new lambs and kid goats. So, verse 35, Laban true to form, thinks he'll pull a fast one on Jake and right away separates all the said adult goats and sheep. His boys move them three days away. He thinks this will make it tuff for Jake to raise a flock. Verses 35 and 36.

III. But ya CAN'T pull a fast one on God who's behind it all.

A. Verses 37 to 39. Ol' Jake was a herdsman of herdsmen: a notch above most. God blessed him with the desire and ability to notice certain characteristics concerning the animals throwing kids and lambs. Likewise, he could select the stronger sheep and goats and keep them separate from the weaker ones. Verse 40. All these, of course, were blessed by God as God promised.

1. The idea of putting the various wood in the watering troughs may produce a chemical that makes the females come into heat quickly. Therefore, he could control the breeding process for the stronger critters — breed when he wanted them to, whereas the weaker would breed less. Whether or not stripping the wood induces spotted and striped offspring, I couldn't say. But God would provide. Whether Jake knew this fully or not, I don't know. But as God controls the womb of women, likewise He controls the wombs of critters too.

2. Jake recognized these solid colored critters still threw spotted and dark young. As well as he stated in verse 30, "the Lord has blessed" Laban through Jake's effort and knew God would bless him now.

3. Verse 42. The weaker seemed to throw solid colors. So, Jake's flocks grew in numbers; vigorous, strong animals, hence very marketable. With Jake's management skill and business sense, he became, in short order, wealthy. Verse 43.

All this is ACCORDING to the Providence of God. (Pre-arrangement's purpose in His-Story.) Likewise, we need to seek to recognize this truth in our part in His-Story. Now please be praying for Noray in Mongolia. His particular ministry is working with individuals in sports.

He did some kind of high-jump, landed wrong, and a couple days ago said he couldn't move. That's all I know. Maybe, Chim, you could call and let me know. Thanks for taking the time to read this study.

May the Lord Bless you with it, Mike

Question for Discussion

1. Seeing how Laban was, we see much of the world is like that. We are to show honesty, yet we need to be wary of the world today. How should we apply Matthew 10:16 in our dealings with the world?

God Tells Jacob It's Time to Go Home

Mornin' folks. It's been a while since we've looked at Ol' Jake. We've had family here for two and a half weeks, but we're here alone now. Still a little tuckered out caring for all them, but it was good! Hope you all been Blessed by God in our absence.

Let's pray.

Genesis 31:1–20 KJV

I. Laban's plan to multiply his herd at Jake's expense. It didn't turn out, for God was with Jake and Laban's not friendly.

A. Verses 1 and 2. When a crafty man plans to take advantage of someone, and it doesn't turn out, they get bitter. So it was with Laban's boys, as well as Laban.

B. Verse 3. What Jake was waiting for finally came. God calls on Jacob and tells Him head on home; it's time. (Back to the land of thy fathers, Abe and Ike.) Again, God assures him I WILL BE WITH YOU! Jacob understands it's been God caring for him and seems to be trusting Him more and more.

II. Jake tests the waters, so to speak. He explains to his wives what's been going on and what God said.

A. Verses 4 to 8. He gets them in private to explain that

their dad isn't friendly anymore for his herd is getting smaller while ours is getting larger. The God of my fathers has been with me; that's why our herds increase. I've worked hard and honestly for your dad all these years; you know that, right? But your father has changed our agreement ten times trying to stop me from gaining a large herd. Yet God continued to change what lambs and kids would come to match the color in which Laban changed the agreement. Ol' Laban and his boys are "ticked-off!"

1. Verse 9. God has taken from your dad and given to me.
   a. Verses 10 to 13. Jake explains how God did intervene; how in a dream Jake had, God explained even though his rams and billies were solid in color, yet in the dream, he saw speckled and ring-shaped climb on the ewes. This meant God will give the power of those rams and billies to have the color that Laban said Jake could have at the time. Got it? That's what happened.
   b. As well as God let him know He saw (Angel of God) all that Laban had done to Jake. This is Christ, God the Son. (Remember Genesis 16:9 and also see 48:16) God reminds Jake, "I'm the God you vowed the Vow to." (I think God may be saying you've done well, but that's just a thought, don't know for sure.) The vow was to declare Jake will now worship the God of his fathers. (A tenth given for an offering. I wonder what and how he gave that? It doesn't say, does it?)

  c. So, after explaining all this, Jake says God has told me it's time to go home. What will the little ladies say?

III. The girls reply, "Let's get outta Dodge!"

  A. Verses 14 to16. What we had with our father is finished. We go with you. "Whatsoever, God said unto you, DO!"

  B. Verses 17 and 18. So, they put on the big skedaddle. This is a camel train! All their outfit is put on these critters with the kids on top. Their servants are herding their sheep and goats. Quite a scene to see these herdsmen travel. Whether or not Jake's sneaking out on Laban was right or in faith, I can't say. But as we'll see, God was protecting him in this move He told Jacob to make.

   1. Verse 19. Just because Jake believed in the true God doesn't mean the love of his life did. Rachel takes her Ol' Pa's idols, little toy-size figures. Those people put them on a shelf in their houses or tents for protection and good luck. Some think she did it so they could claim any inheritance that they might get. I think she was hanging onto them in belief and may not have believed in the true God, or just mixed the faith in both. (Colossians 2:8)
   2. Verse 20. Jake's herd was away from the herds of Laban so it would be easy for Jake to leave without Laban knowing for a few days.

I think we'll stop here, but we see Jake, in faith, trusted God; we should too. I think when Jake first really recognized he could trust God was at the well in Genesis 29:1–12. He'll have some ups and very big downs, but we'll

see in the end he makes it into the "Faith Hall of Fame."
(Hebrews 11)

Have a blessed week! Mike

Question for Discussion

1. Colossians 2:8 is a good verse with which to look at ourselves. It's so easy for us to ignore considering what we do day to day without asking ourselves, is it pleasing to God? And the things we do in the Church without considering if they are from man or from God's word.

Laban's Hot but God Warns Him Jacob's Mine

Mornin' folks. Let's keep ridin' this bronc tills she's done.

Let's pray.

Genesis 31:21–55 KJV

I. So, Jacob "sets his face towards Mount Gilead."

    A. Verse 21. Jake, with all his livestock and outfit, found a crossing. My experience crossing big rivers is you gotta cross um where they're widest. It's not as deep, and current's not as bad. With the size of Jake's caravan, the crossing will take some time. But once across, he could put on "the big skedaddle." But again, with their moving a herd and outfit that size, 15 miles a day would be good.

        1. Mt Gilead is really the hilly country east of the Jordan River. Later in Exodus, you'll see Gad, Reuben, and half of the Manasseh tribes want this country cause of the good grazing. So, this country was good for Jake's outfit. But it's about a 300-mile trail. They'll kill sheep and goats as they go for grub, as well as they have to milk the goats, morning and night. They graze some as they go, but they'll have to graze at night too. There's a learning that Jake's life has taught him.

Herdsmen ain't no "creampuffs." They're savvy folks. Mongol herdsmen were like this. Don't come any tuffer, and Ol' Jake was tuff.

B. Verse 22. Laban hears three days later that Jake ran off with what was rightfully Jacob's, but Laban was like the street, one way. He was ticked-off. He figured he'd somehow cheat Jake out of what Jake got from being a smart herdsman. Besides, he's the boss of this family, not Jake (his thinkin'). On top of that, all his family household gods were missing! So, he saddles his camel, Clyde, and rides! (I don't know the name of Laban's camel, but that rhymes.) He takes some of his men because they're planning to take it all back and maybe kill Jake if need be. It took them seven days to catch up, so Jake has been on the trail ten days with maybe a 60-mile head-start on Laban. Those goats and sheep must have moved faster than I thought possible cause Laban catches up to Jake in Gilead. Verse 23. 300 miles in ten days now that's whippin' and a spurrin'! (Their livestock are tired and hungry, but they're at Gilead.)

II. God straightens Laban out before they catch up to Jake.

A. Here in Verses 23, 24, and 25, they're close to Jake's outfit; perhaps see their camp but bed down for the night. Then God stepped into Laban's sleep and put the fear of God in him. "Jake's mine and you'd do well to watch your step around what is mine. You've been warned!" (I don't know what he said to Laban but as we'll see Laban heeds His warning!)

1. So now Laban goes to face Jacob. Verses 26 to 29. He starts out like he's hurt that he couldn't send off his loved ones with the proper blessings

and good-byes. But the fact is, he wants all that Jake has and was using this as an excuse to take what Jake had. But God stepped in and put fear into Laban's heart. After trying to make Jake ashamed for sneaking out like he did, Laban confesses he's scared to harm Jake in any way. (Verse 29. I have the power to do you hurt.) The "God of Jacob's fathers" warned him not to say anything that would cause trouble. Truth is, if Laban could have, he'd have taken everything and was mad enough to perhaps kill Jake. He really probably cared more for all that Jake had than for his daughters and grandkids. Good-bye. But it sounded good that he felt slighted about not being able to give a going away party. (Liar!)

2. Then like he's an understanding father-in-law, he says, "I know you want to be with your folks, but why did ya steal my gods!" Verse 30. Jake doesn't know anything about it. Says, "Search and see who has them, and you can kill who took them." Verses 31 and 32. We know who took them; we read it in verse 19, but they don't. Laban searches everyone's tent. It's interesting that they all had different tents and didn't sleep together. Verses 33 to 35. Rachel was a sly one; she hid them on her camel's saddle which also served as a kind of couch in her tent. When her father came in, she explained her not standing in the presence of her father as she was having her monthlies, her period of blood coming out. That satisfied him. His gods couldn't be found! It's interesting, God allows things like this and then tells us no more about it.

III. Now it's Jacob's time to get mad, and he tells it like it is!

A. Verses 36 to 42. After 20 years of subjecting himself to this selfish, conniving, hypocrite, and Laban finding no fault to tack on Jake to justify his hot pursuit; Jake BLOWS UP!

1. Verse 37. You came after me like I was a thief! What have you found that I stole! (Laban found nothing.)
2. Verse 38. Laban lost no lambs or kids cause of Jake's careful shepherding, and furthermore, Jake never took from Laban's flock to eat.
3. Verse 39. As for wild critters killing your sheep, I took the loss and gave you mine! If any were stolen; I took the loss!
4. Verse 40. "Laban, I worked hard for you in the heat of day and cold of night. I always worked hard for you! I lost sleep! I always did a good job!" I think I'd a said few more choice words and maybe of thrown a punch. God forgive me! But Jake was a cool customer. He kept himself in control, thanks be to God!
5. Verse 41. "On top of all this, you changed our deal ten times seeking to cheat me!"
6. "But GOD!" Verse 42. "God made the ewes and nannies throw the color you changed my wage to each time He protected me! The God of Abraham and the God who my father Isaac feared. (Laban you'd do well to fear him too is my thought.) He's the one who rebuked you yesterday!" (Ol' Laban is a real special case!)

B. Laban is as slippery as a snake and replies in verse 43, "Aw Jake, do you really think I'd a hurt my girls or grandkids? Look at all you have; it started with Ol' Laban. So, come on. Let's make a covenant. You stay on your side of the fence, and I'll stay on mine! What'd ya say, SON!?" (Ol' Laban is slick.) Apologizing ain't in his make up! As I said, he's like the street – one way! A good example of 2 Timothy 2:25, no one can repent but by God granting it. "Peradventure God gives them repentance unto the ACKNOWLEDGEMENT of the TRUTH!" Even we are in need of God's grace to repent. (Romans7:15,22,23) Apart from God, we are all a sorry bunch! I guess this can be the application of this story for us.

IV. So, the outcome is, let's make a border between us. You stay on your side of the fence. I'll stay on mine, so to speak.

   A. Verses 44 to 47. Laban says, "Let's make a covenant." (As if Jake trusts Laban.) So, Jake agrees and builds a "marker" with his men. Then they cooked some grub and ate with Laban's bunch of "scallywags" that "bona fides" the agreement. Verse 46.

     1. These rocks are known as "heap of witness." Verse 47. Laban calls in Aramaic and Jake in Hebrew, but the place was thereon known as Galeed, another name for heap of witness. Verse 48. (Witness between me and you.)

     2. Verse 49. "Mizpah," meaning watchtower. "The Lord watch between me and you."

        a. Ol' Laban, he's got to try and put the monkey on Jake's back and starts adding threats to this. As if Jake's a bad guy and he's a sweetheart. "You be warned. Don't you hurt my girls or take any other wives or God will cruse you. You swear God is witness."

        b. Verse 51. Laban, true to form, says, "I have cast this agreement between us, you are warned" He takes the credit. (He's a slick one.)

    c. Verse 53. Laban tries to mix up, combine his little gods with the true God. It's the word "Elohim" plural gods. But Jake's not slow in the head and does it right "in the fear of Isaac," the True and only God whom his father worships.

B. Verses 54 and 55. Jake finishes this deal with worship of God and His Promise and sacrifices to God. They all eat and that unsaved man, Laban heads home never to be heard of again.

This episode of Jacob's life is over. He's now back in the Promised Land, and the trail of the "Seed of the Woman" continues.

Have a blessed week! Mike

Preparing to Meet His Brother, Fear Strikes Jacob. He Calls on God; Later Wrestles with God and His Name is Changed to Israel

Mornin' folks. It's Monday and a beautiful day on "Me Island." Let's see if we can get another study done this week. Next week we'll have a young pastor (he's a Mexican Indian) and his wife and two daughters here for ten days. He will be the main speaker at the tent meeting that's going on in the Indian Reservation on our Lake. "Vermilion Waters" is the name of our little fellowship group. Lord willing one day a Church. It'll run 8/7 to 8/9.

Let's pray.

Genesis 32:1–32 KJV

I. He camps with Angels.

A. Verses 1 and 2. Here his caravan is a day or few from where he and Laban built the boundary between them and called it "Mizpah" (God watch over this). Now it's toward evening, and they're about to camp. God pulls apart the veil between the Physical world and the Spiritual world, and Jacob sees Angels of God. It doesn't say if anyone else saw these Angels or not. But Jake did, so he names the place, "Mahanaim" (where two companies camped).

1. This is like the time at Bethel on his way to find his mother's brother Laban, where in a dream he saw the Angels. Here it seems this was not a dream. He recognized God was with him. But Jake's about to meet his brother Esau. The way it was when he left home, Esau wanted him dead. His mother said she'd send word when it was safe to come home and so far, she hadn't. So even though God said to go home, he wasn't sure what to expect. This is like the time with Elisha in 2 Kings 6:16–18 when Syrian troops were coming for him. His servant was afraid, so Elisha asked God to reveal the troops of Heaven to his servant to calm his fear. Jake should feel safe, but will he?

II. Jacob prepares to meet his brother, Esau.

A. Verses 3 to 8. So, as we read this, we see he sends a troop of messengers to Edom. It appears to be about 100-miles south and to the east of the Dead Sea. They probably went with camels, but still, it would have been maybe a week or ten days before they brought word back. So, Jake's camped on a creek called Jabrook that flows into the Jordan River from the East about 24-miles north of the mouth. Jacob waits with all his livestock and outfit.

1. Verse 6. The messengers come back with not a clear feel of brother Esau's intentions. He's coming to meet Jake with 400 of his men!
2. This erases Faith in God and puts fear in Jake's heart! Verse 7. He divides his company into two companies with the idea if one is attacked, the other might get away, maybe. Verse 8.

B. Verses 9 to 12. Jake comes to his senses and cries out to God! He is doing what we see many times the New Testament reminds us to do. Cast your cares on Him for He cares for you. (1 Peter 5:7 and Philippians 4:6 are examples.) As Abe learned he could absolutely Trust God's word, so will Jake in time learn to trust Him fully as well. So, Jake's really doing what he should, cast his cares on Him. This is a good lesson for us when we fear to tell Him. Notice he's retelling God's promises to him. This is good, it reminds us what He did say, and we should trust Him even when it looks bad. Those 21 Egyptian Christians who got their heads cut off, it appeared they had faith in what God promised them as to where they'll go. This is a good lesson for us as Romans 15:4 says, God, CAN be trusted! As we'll see, it will all work out. His-Story was written in His mind before He created the Heavens and the Earth. He gave an Oath in Isaiah14:24. God help me to Believe this even MORE! In His Name, Amen.

1. Verse 10. Notice Jake confesses the truth about himself. I hope we recognize this in ourselves. He's done what he thinks best dividing his outfit in two camps and now looks to the Lord for His promised protection and Blessings.
2. Verse 11. He comes right out and asks the Lord, deliver me from the hands of my brother! He admits he is afraid of his brother. This is such an honest, straightforward, prayer-example of what we should do in the valleys of our lives. Then he asks for reassurance. Verse 12. Lord you promised me, my father, and my grandfather that our Seed would be many, but it sure looks like it could all end soon! Lord, I'm struggling with the circumstances of my life to not to overcome my Faith!

C. The struggle continues in Jake's mind, for he thinks, maybe I can soften Esau's heart with gifts of livestock. Verses 13 to 16. He then instructed his herdsmen as to what to say to his brother in verses 17 to 20.

1. Notice back in verse 15 where it's said 40 kine? That's cows or young heifers along with ten bulls. I thought earlier he had just sheep and goats? Where did all the cows come from? Must have bought them before they left Haran country?

III. Night has come but still worried; then comes face to face with our Lord, God.

A. Verse 21. The gift is the livestock for Esau, and he sent that on ahead; probably the way Esau would be coming. The rest of his outfit stayed put for the night, but Jake himself is restless (verses 22 to 24) and starts out taking his four wives and kids across the creek Jabbok. If the commentators are right, this crossing is four miles from the mouth where it flows into the Jordan River. By the way, this name has a meaning of "to wrestle;" probably it got this name after this episode. But it seems Jacob in the night decided to move his whole outfit across, and then he stayed by himself. Verse 24. "And Jacob was left alone." (How that all went down is not totally clear.) The main thing is Jake's alone now and is in serious prayer to God.

B. Still, in verse 24, the prayer became real! He is confronted with a man who fights with him. They are wrestling all night.

1. Verse 25. This man can't get Jacob off him, so he touches Jake's hip bone and dislocates it.

2. Verse 26. Even with the awful pain of a dislocated hip, Jake won't let go and says it's getting daylight. Let go! Here we know this isn't just a man, but God, more than likely Christ in human form for Jake says, "No! Not until you bless me!"
3. Verses 27 and 28. Angel of God (we'll say he's this for it seems when in the Old Testament it's understood to be Christ) asks what's your name, knowing full well who he's wrestling with. In verse 28, our Lord says, "You are no longer 'heal grabber,' but the Prince that has power with God and man and has prevailed – ISRAEL."
4. Verse 29. Israel asks, "What's your name?" God here answers back, "why do ya ask?" meaning you know who I AM, or you wouldn't ask me to Bless ya! Then He did bless him right there and then.
5. Verse 30. We see here Israel knows this was God, and he saw God face to face, and his life was spared! So, He called the place Penuel – "the face of God."
6. Verse 31. It's morning now, and Israel crosses the creek to his camp with a limp. God made that happen so he would know this was real, not a dream. His family would know this too, that what he said did happen. Verse 32. We see they made a law not to eat that part of the meat where the hip joint is.

This is an important meeting, not just for Israel but for us to see with the persistence of prayer according to the will of God; God will acknowledge us in a relationship manner. They of old didn't fully recognize the Son as we do on this side of the Cross. The blessing that came to Jacob (Israel) was forwarded to us and is now fully recognized as "Grace" in the person of Jesus the Christ. The blessing that Jacob received was passed down to us, Grace, which we have received, and as we've received Grace, so we have received Mercy. Therefore, we Faint not! (Hebrews 4:15–16)

Have a Blessed Week! Mike

Questions for Discussion

1. Jacob, now Israel, has fear. He knows God said, go home. But then his momma never said to come yet. So, there was that nagging question, can I really trust God? Israel gets serious with petitions to God. He gets alone and confesses his fear and wants reassurance. There should be times in our lives where we have had and will be confronted with things that have the potential to get real bad for us. What do you think of what Jacob did? Did it work?
2. We saw here in this study that this was what God said to do. Right? The problem may not go away, but we still need to go forward, trusting even when we can't understand the whys and wherefores of it all. Do we need to? What does the Shield of Faith represent in Ephesians 6:16?

The Reunion with Esau Turns from Fear to Joy!

Mornin' folks. Hope this finds you blessed and thankful. We were blessed with a God-led tent meeting, our second for Vermilion Waters Fellowship. Good messages, testimonies, blessed singing, and fellowship. A couple who had been living together for years were convicted; got married there. Still, those lost in this village here didn't come. We advertised it well, and those who God brought were Blessed. Thank you, Lord. Let's see what God teaches us this week.

Let's pray.

Genesis 33:1–20 KJV

I. The time with the Lord is passed and, in the morning, Jacob sees Esau coming.

A. Verses 1 to 7. Now is the meeting. Jake still doesn't know for sure what to expect, yet God said, again and again, I'm with you. So, he quickly arranges his family in the order of his favored wives and children. Rachel being most loved he puts in back. Verse 2. (Unfortunately, this favoritism will cause much pain in the future even though God will use that for His purpose.)

1. Verse 3 says Jake ran forward of his family to meet his brother and as he went to him, he bowed himself seven times. Apparently, in those days

when you come to a King, that's what you do in respect of the King. Here Jake is recognizing Esau as the Lord of that land which he was, of Edom. Esau was able to gather 400 men. It would seem to understand his Lordship, as well as I'm sure travelers have brought news. The family of Isaac was famous.

2. Verse 4. His worries were unfounded. God had worked a work in Esau; his heart reconciled to the fact that even if he had not the Blessing of his father, things were as they were, and he was blessed. His love for his brother was important. They both wept openly on each other. Twenty years of dread meeting his brother, I'm sure drained him, and the emotions of relief were great. God was indeed with him as promised working things out for His purpose. (How many times has something like this happened to me, and my worries were for not? I seem to be a slow study on such. I'm sure you do a better job of trusting than I do.)

3. Verses 5 to 7. Esau is introduced to Jake's family. "Kids, meet your uncle, Esau." Jake says, "this is the family God blessed me with," and the wives paid respect to Esau.

II. What's all these livestock heading my way?

A. Verses 8 to 11. Back then, and even in more recent times, to one desiring reconciliation, you first sent a gift. If it's accepted, then you go forward to offer reconciliation. Here Jake does this. We see in Esau's thinking it is not necessary, but Jake insists. Finally, to acknowledge Esau accepts reconciliation, he takes the gift. They're both rich in livestock and servants.

1. Verse 10. "Seeing your face is like I've seen the face of God, and you were pleased with me." The joy of finding love instead of wrath was overwhelming like I've seen God's face and lived! He recognizes God's faithfulness in the work he did in Esau's heart toward him. I'm not saying God saved Esau, but just the change He made in Esau's feelings toward Jacob.

III. The reunion seems to be short. Whether they camp together for a while or not, isn't said.

A. Verses 12 to 16. Esau suggests they travel together. But Jake declines. It seems he's really not in a hurry to go see his folks, as well as he's got young livestock and needs to take it slow. He'd pushed them too hard coming from Uncle Laban. Then Esau wants to leave some men with him, probably for protection, but Jake again says gracefully, "Thanks, but no thanks. We'll be just fine." It says Esau departed that same day (short reunion!).

B. Verses 17 to 20. Show Jake's not in a hurry to go anywhere. In fact, he doesn't cross over the Jordan but throws up a house and makes sheds and corrals for the stock at a place not far away called Succoth. This is interesting to me cause it's like he thinks he'll stay there. Probably that country was good grass so, as herdsmen are not too worried about time, stayed there a good spell. Perhaps as long as ten years. Succoth means booths or shelters.

IV. It's time to cross the Jordan to the Promised Land!

A. Verse 18. So, he "heads 'um up; moves 'um out" (gets his livestock moving), crosses the Jordan and takes his outfit to a main town of the Canaanites. It's in hill country north of Jerusalem (although Jerusalem wasn't there then), about 30 miles. They came in peace to that city and appeared not to have problems with the people there. He's back in his tent now (enough of those walls). This is the land God promised Abraham, Isaac, and he, Israel.

1. Verses 19 and 20. Shechem is run by a fella named Hamor. Israel buys a piece of land from him. This, by the way, is where Abe first built an altar, and God met him here in Canaan. Israel sets up camp there. It cost him 100 pieces of silver (not sure what that would be worth today). It had to be a sizeable piece cause his outfit was real big, probably a hundred people I'd guess, plus livestock.

2. Verse 20. Here's the good part. Israel worships his God, the True God of Heaven and Earth in the middle of a pagan land. He builds an altar and names it A Mighty God, The God of Israel! Not the altar but the God he worships.

The "Seed of the Woman" that Jacob is transporting is back in the land that was promised his people. Israel sees God kept His word. He is with him and can be trusted. The land is bought, this is his country, and here God is worshiped.

Blessings, Mike

Thought to consider – Ah . . . relief, the greatest feeling known to man! Get it?

A Dark Time for the Family

Mornin' folks, Finally, got some rain here. It's been dry but not hot; just right. We got through chapter 33, and now we're following Jacob's family's life in the promised land. Here we'll come to a dark spot in Jacob's family. We'll get through this whole chapter in this study.

Let's pray.

Genesis 34:1–31 KJV

I. Dinah wants some girlfriends and gets in trouble.

A. It seems as we saw in the last study, Jacob's family probably hung out in Succoth for around maybe ten years then moved to near Shechem. Now, Canaan, is an idolatress land perhaps morally similar to Sodom but not yet to that extreme. Nonetheless, Jake has twelve boys and Dinah by four wives. That alone is hard to manage, but they're mainly busy taking care of their livestock. The twelve boys probably enjoy each other (maybe), but Dinah wants some girlfriends. So, in verse 1, we see she goes looking for some in Shechem. Then the trouble comes. She seems to be a looker and probably around 14 or 15-years-old. Verse 2. Shechem is the name of the town and also the name of the son of the Lord of Shechem, Hamor. Shechem, the son, saw Dinah and lusted for her. Whether it was consent or outright rape, it doesn't say but in the eyes of God, and this God-following family, she was violated. The people of this land held that an unattached lady was fair game to have sex with; in fact, it was in their religion (part of Baal worship). Hamor was a Hivite. Seems the Hivites were scattered throughout Canaan. Remember he was the sixth son of Canaan. In this land of Canaan, there's Hivites, Amorites, etc. that were all Canaanite.

1. Shechem, after his lust, fell in love with Dinah, verse 3, and took her home. Whether she went willingly or not isn't said, so don't know if Dinah felt the same way. But in verse 4, he asks his dad to go approach Jacob about marrying Dinah. In Israel's thinking (which was from God) the sexual act was after the parents had agreed to the marriage and it was by an oath. We come to verses 5 to 7 and how seriously all of Israel took this matter of rape, whether Dinah consented or not. The sex was done without marriage to their daughter and sister. Notice in verse 7 it says, "Which thing ought not to be done." They were more than a little angry as you'll see.

II. Hamor and Shechem come to Israel to seek Dinah's hand for Shechem.

A. Verses 8 to12. Back in verse 5, Jake was alone so he wouldn't say anything, but then his boys came, and when they heard, they were Hot! Their whole family name is shamed by this. (I'm sure they're thinking vengeance then.)

B. Hamor starts in about what he came to bargain about, and that was to give Shechem Dinah to marry. In those times, even the Pagans saw marriage as an agreement between the two family heads. But Hamor's thinking is the economic value his family would receive. (Verse10)

1. At this point, the boy in love can't hold back anymore. Verses 11 and12. He'll do anything for Dinah's hand. "Anything, but give me Dinah!"

C. So here we see Jacob keeping quiet, and his boys do the bargaining. Verses 13 to 17. Several of these boys of Jake's are maybe in their late twenties. Notice verse 13, they answered "deceitfully." It seems they've got a plan of vengeance.

1. We'll see, as time gets us further into Genesis, these boys are turning into men. They aren't any spiritual sweethearts; they're mostly mean, bitter and jealous without the mercy we saw in Abe or the recognition of God leading and blessing them as their father Jacob showed.

2. Verses 14 to 17. Jacob seems not to say anything and the boys seem to be quick thinkin' (of course God is behind this good or bad). Whether they had a "Focsil Council" (a private talk between themselves as to what they wanted) and then came back with their terms, or they just thought it up as they were listening to Hamor, or because God made a decree to Abraham that they were to be separate people and the circumcision was the mark to distinguish them, they replied like this. "You have to be like us if we're going to join our families together or we'll leave and take Dinah. The choice is yours!"

D. Verses 19 to 24. Well, here we go. They agree to this thing, this painful circumcision. They think they'll get Israel's livestock and wealth by joining. All but Shechem. Look at verse 19, Shechem was more honorable than the rest of them. Meaning he was respected in his city, a man that could be trusted, probably kind. (God's grace is even on the unsaved remember, as to what level of morality He intends for them. They'll only fall as far into wickedness as God allows for His purpose for them or He'll let them fall. Romans1:24,26,28) So Shechem talked them into agreeing to this PAINFUL thing! Ouch! At the city gates, they all did this.

1. Notice Hamor's motive, verse 23. He planned on getting all that Israel had, and that made the men motived to do this painful act.

2. Verse 24. We see they agreed to this thing, and so now the pain begins! It's so bad, as we'll see, they can't move enough to defend themselves. I read where the third day is the height of the pain for such a surgery.

III. Shechem tried to make things right, but the wrathful vengeance of Dinah's brothers could not be satisfied.

A. Verses 25 and 26. Remember, as it said in verse 13, this was done deceitfully. It appears this was planned out to get the whole city defenseless. Now I'm sure this isn't just a handful of men in Shechem but at least hundreds. As we look back to Genesis 29:32–35, Leah had four sons Reuben, Simeon, Levi, and Judah. But here we see only Simeon and Levi attacked the city. Why? All four were Dinah's full brothers, yet only the two that were recorded went in. Now I'd bet they had servants that went too; however, none of that was recorded. They went through the whole city, killing all the males. That's not a small job of butchery with a sword!

1. Let's stop and consider God here. This isn't the last bad thing these boys do, yet God has elected these to be under His Grace. Levi's seed will eventually become God's Priests for Israel. Go to Deuteronomy 9:4–6 and remember all man is wicked and if God chooses one bunch of wicked men to take what another bad bunch has, it is God's sovereign choice, pre-ordained to be so. If God allows this to happen, first, the victims deserve it, and second, if He allowed this, He then intended it to happen because nothing can be done unless God intends it to be. Nothing, absolutely nothing!

2. However, Simeon and Levi were punished by God through their father. (Genesis 49:5–7). Simeon's descendants were given land inside Judah's inheritances. Levi didn't get any, but later stood apart from the golden calf incident in Exodus and didn't participate. Therefore, God made them Priests of Israel. Here it sounds like these two men did all the butchery.

3. They worked their way to Shechem's home and mercilessly slaughtered Shechem and Hamor. They took their sister back. I'm wondering if she wanted back or not? It doesn't say.

   a. Here we need to think fornication was accepted by these people while God hates this sin. (1 Corinthians 6:18) God says this is the worst sin, and obviously these sons and Israel reckoned this the same to where this kind of hate would only be relieved by murder. (1 John3:15) Both these sins, fornication and hate, are in man. What man doesn't have these? Yet a man Born-Again in Christ knows it is sin, and fears and is tormented with these inner struggles. Whereas men of Canaan, or of the world, have no fear or shame. God rejected these people of Shechem. They're in hell awaiting the Lake of Eternal Fire.

C. Now the greed overcomes ALL the sons of Israel. They come in and plunder the city, taking for themselves women and children, livestock and riches, and weapons of war. They were no different from the rest of the world. Verses 27 to 29. The women and children were slaves now of Israel. Israel is a huge company, a village wandering where the grass is green. Yet nothing bad was said about this plunder. I'm sure there was fornication by the sons of Israel with these slave women. Yet, nothing is said of this. However, . . .

1. Verse 30. Jacob says, "Look at what you did. We'll be hated and attacked by all the people of this land!" He seems to forget, "but God." He promised Jake He'd be with him. He won't let anything happen to him. As we'll see later, God will punish Simeon and Levi's seed for this bloody thing.
2. Verse 31. It seems Jake was silenced by the question, "Is our sister to be treated like a

whore?" Jake didn't do anything to deal with this sin against his daughter. That seemed to shut him up.

A thought: when we get too close to the world, we can expect trouble. His children do not have as close a relationship as Jacob has with the Lord. We'll see that in the future. They're not much different from the Canaanites. Sin always confuses things, and this whole chapter is confusing. It just ends with nothing else said till chapter 49.

This is a good reason for us to dwell on Romans 12:19 and teach our kids in the hope God will grant them repentance from taking vengeance when wronged by others. It's not easy in this world, and it won't get better! BUT! Then we have eternal Life through Jesus Christ, our Lord! God understands this confusion, and we trust Him to straighten it out. We have hope in Him!

Blessings, to ya! Mike

Lord! Revive My Family!

Mornin' folks. Today is Tuesday and yesterday we got chapter 34 out, so now I'll study some chapter 35. See when it gets finished.

Let's pray.

Genesis 35:1–15 KJV

I. God speaks to Jacob again

A. They'd been among the heathens too long, and trouble came. I'm thinkin' Jake got a little comfortable and let things slide some, which we do when we get too comfortable in the world. A lot of Idol worship there: bad luck, good luck, thinking. Copper Indians call it "Ingee," certain things you do certain ways or bad luck comes on you. That's generally part of idolatry. In Mongoland the Buddhists had to go serve tea to the spirits before anyone could drink tea, so mom would take a cup outside, and as I remember, throw it up in the air then come in and then we could drink some. Things like that and their little statues had to have some tea in front of them too.

Here, in Jake's household, he was a little careless and ignored some of his wife's idol trinkets (Rachel stole some from her Dad remember) and perhaps some of their servants also had some, and they lived near Shechem a long time, so I'm sure there was some influence as well. God in verse 1 says to get outta' Dodge. Go up to the place you really started with Me and begin again! (1 Peter 1:15)

1. In verse 2, we see Jake tells all his people to give him all their idol trinkets and such; we're gonna get right with the TRUE God! We're going to the House of God! (Bethel, that's the meaning.) At that time it was called Luz but would be known later as the "House of God," Bethel. This is where God came to Jacob in the dream with the stairs that angels were going up and down from heaven. Chapter 28. They were to change their clothes and not wear garments that the heathens wore anymore and to clean themselves; symbolic of purity. Begin again! They were going Home so to speak! Like going to see their Father, the King, which He is! How much Jake has taught his family about the God of his fathers, I know not, but probably not as much as he should and later it will show with his boys. (Yet God does the Electing).

2. Nonetheless, they obeyed Jake's command and gave him all their idol things which he buried. Verse 4.

II. So the huge caravan of Israel headed to God's house.

A. Remember, Jake feared the people of the land would attack him. (He forgot God for that moment.) But God, true to His word (verse 5) caused fear to come on all their neighbors. They, in all the time in Canaan, never were attacked in any way. God shows us time, and again He will care for His Elect, which also you and I are. As we saw Abe, Ike, and now Jake, we tend to forget this and fear. I from time to time have too, and if you're not too proud to admit it, you also have. Romans 15:4 keeps coming to mind.

B. Verse 6. So, Israel arrives at the place to begin again. Similar to when Abe ran off to Egypt in Genesis 13:1–4. (Seems like this may even be the same place. If it is, it wouldn't surprise me; God so often does this; a special ground, a Holy place to begin again!) "And ALL the people with him." This is a recognition of the great number of people and family that is under his authority. It doesn't say how many but there could well be over a thousand!

1. Verse 7. Here is the place God visited him when he was on the run from Esau and built an Altar to God. He now does the same, for God was truly always was with him and brought him back to the House of God, Bethel. Then he named this new altar, The STRONG God of Bethel (El-Bethel).

2. Verse 8. Here, someone apparently very special to Jacob's family dies. Genesis 24:59 tells of a nurse that comes along with Rebekah. We learn her name is Deborah. She must have been dear to them for where they buried her is called "Allon-bachuth," oak of weeping.

   a. An interesting note here, whether it's a fact, I can't say, but in a Jewish historian's writing called "The Targum of Johnathan," traditional belief is Deborah was Rebekah's nurse (which it says here). As I said above, there seems to be an idea she may have come to get Jacob and bring him home. Also, Jake's mom dies, but it doesn't say when.

III. God appears to Jacob and restates what He said at the Brook of Jabook.

A. Verses 9 to 15. God appears to Jacob. Now the name for God here is El-Shaddai. "Shad" in Hebrew is breast, apparently meaning the one who nourishes with strength to meet every need. God appears then to be in a form that Jacob could see, and He talks with him and reminds him again what a Blessed possession he and his Seed have. Which should also remind us, the children of the most-High God, joint heirs with Christ, that we should walk in the manner of such a one. (1 Peter 1:15; Ephesians 4:1)

1. Verse 10. Here again, God says you are no longer Jacob but Israel. (Persists with God and prevails. We might say persistent in prayer.) Another Jewish writer says it's really, "you will ALSO be called Israel," and then in the future when his children become a nation, they will be Israel. However, in future chapters he's called Israel and in other places, Jacob. I don't know Hebrew enough to know the purpose of why some places he's called Israel, then others Jacob. I'm sure there is a reason, though. He tells him again here what He already told him about his name change as some commentators said in Jabook when he wrestled with an Angel. Here God makes it official. I'm not sure what they say is correct or not, but nonetheless, it's official now. Israel shall be the family name and one day when they walk across the Red Sea; they will be the nation chosen of God called ISRAEL.

2. Verse 11. He commands Israel to have many children. He's got a good start: twelve boys, one daughter. (Four hundred years later, a couple of million strong). We see twelve tribes of Israel will be that company of nations who God says always WILL BE! And of course, we can't forget

the "Seed of The Woman" will come out of this nation; the Lamb of God who taketh away the sin of the world. Not just King David, but also the King of Kings!

3. Verse 12. God again reaffirms His word of which He reminded Abe and Ike and now Jake many times, "this land. I give to you and yours forever!" In God's thinking, even when they were absent, the land was still theirs, and so it is!

4. Verse 13. God rises up and away in the form that he came and visited Jacob. Perhaps on Jacob's ladder. (Genesis 28:12 and John 1:51) Christ is the Way, as in John 14:6. Nonetheless, He came, said what He intended, and left.

B. Verses 14 and 15. This is what we could call consecrating this place: a special place to worship God. The Mosaic Law wasn't given yet, so this was still as it was handed down from Abe and even Noah. Nonetheless, Jacob did his best to bring honor to the most-High God. As we All should.

Israel is directing his family to begin again to truly worship God alone. We'll see how that goes in future chapters.

Well, have a Blessed week. Until next time, Mike

Question for Discussion

1. A man is the head of a household, right? So, when we see one, or the whole family, drifting toward the ways of the world, what should we do? Idols could be considered anything we might put before God.

"On the Road Again," One Is Born and Two Pass On

Mornin' folks. Monday here. Lotta' smoke from all the fires in the west and in Canada. Last week we saw God directing Israel to repent, you could say begin again to completely worship the true God. Now we come to see they're on the move again and sorrow comes to Israel, as well as another son.

Let's pray.

Genesis 35:16–29 KJV

I. Seems Israel is heading now to go to his father, Isaac.

A. It doesn't say how long they stay there in Bethel, but apparently, Rachel is with child. The road they travel on passes through a village we are familiar with, Bethlehem, where the "Seed of the Woman" also known as "The Son of God" was born. It was called Ephrath in the olden days, and here Rachel has another son. Verse 1.

1. Back in Genesis 30:24 it says Rachel prophesied she would have another son and so she does now; about 15 years after Joseph was born. Jake is maybe 105-years-old. I'm thinkin' Rachel is 45 to 50 depending on how old she was when Jake came to Laban. Let's add up the years. Jake went to Uncle Laban and stayed there twenty years. Then between time spent in Succoth, She-

chem, and Bethel perhaps another eleven years. Now they are near Bethlehem, 36 years later, give or take a few. It's hard to figure out the time and exact age of these folks. I've gone to a study about the age of several in Genesis, and I'll try to explain this in the next study. For now, we'll use this as the timeline.

2. Verses 17 and 18. We see she has a tuff delivery. Probably she tore something and bled out for she dies here. Knowing she's about to die she names this son Ben-oni – son of sorrow but in passing Jacob renames him Benjamin – son of the Right Hand signifying a place of honor. The woman he loved has died. I'm sure the sorrow is strong.

3. Verses 18 and 19. Jacob buries Rachel a short way out from Bethlehem. He sets up a monument which was still there when Moses wrote this about four hundred plus years later. I'm sure Jake mourned the loss of his Beloved Wife greatly.

II. Israel still doesn't seem to be in a hurry to get to his father Isaac, and sin finds its way in Israel.

A. So, he stops again. "Spreads his tent" seems to mean he's gonna hang his hat here. How long that is, it doesn't say. Verse 21. The place is called the "Tower of Edar." Actually, it says beyond the Tower of Edar. Beyond is the key. How far from Bethlehem and where Rachel was buried it doesn't say. This tower is also called the Tower of the Flock. It was used as a watch tower for enemies that might steal their flocks. There could have been more than one. Obviously, in Moses' time, they knew exactly where this was. But most common-taters (a little joke) say it was near Bethlehem. How many days south he went no one knows, but Jake's not puttin' on the big skedaddle to see his Ol' Pa.

B. While he camped there a while, some sinful romance starts up, verse 22, between an old lady, Bilhah and Jacob's oldest son, Reuben. Bilhah is the mother of two of Jake's sons, Dan and Naphtali. They seem to be having sex and were caught. Jake, at the time, doesn't punish either of them, yet later in Genesis 49:3–4 we see the birthright was taken away from Reuben. To whom it was given, we'll study later. Bilhah was considered Jacob's property with whom to have sex, his "concubine." The sin seemed to have been stopped but nothing else is said till chapter 49.

C. Verses 22 to 26. All of the beginnings of the Twelve Tribes of Israel are now born. They are recognized again.

1. Leah's boys are Reuben, Simeon, Levi, and Judah. Later Issachar and Zebulun (also Dinah).
2. Rachel's boys are Joseph, and the youngest son, Benjamin.
3. Bilhah's boys are Dan and Naphtali
4. Zilpah boys are Gad and Asher
   a. There are the Twelve Tribes of Israel in the beginning; the twelve sons of Jacob. All according to God's providence (pre-arrangement).

III. Jacob finally gets to Isaac and seems to be with him when he dies.

A. This section is sketchy at best. It may be that Joseph has already been sold into slavery by his brothers. It also doesn't say anything about Jacob's welcoming to his father's tent or how much time he spent with Isaac before his death. It's hard to figure the years it's very confusing.

I'll attempt to deal with them next study when we look at Esau's passing. Nonetheless, in verses 27 to 29, we hear about Ike's death. Nothing is ever mentioned about Rebekah's death. Only that her nurse had died, which may mean Rebekah has died already. We need to keep in mind this is just an overview, it's not a blow by blow account of all that went on back then.

1. Verse 27. So, Jake gets to Abe's Ol' stompin' ground, "The Plains of Mamre" (Genesis 13) also known as Hebron. Now there's a city there called Arbah.
2. In verse 28, we see Ike is 180. Five years older than his Ol' Pa when he died.
3. And we see in verse 29 that Esau came and helped Jacob to bury their father. One generation after another passes away. Hebrews 9:27–28 would be good to remember at this point, as well as Hebrews 11:13–16. Their faith was in God's eternal Promise through the promise of the "Seed of the Woman," Jesus the Christ, as is ours.

Well, may you all have a Blessed week! Mike

Esau and his Nation of Edom

Mornin' folks. This chapter is a little dry and generations are a little confusing, but it's put in the study, so we'll go through it as best we can.

Let's pray.

Genesis 36:1–43 KJV

I. Like Lot and Abraham, they had too much livestock for them to stay together in the same land.

A. Verse 1. This chapter is all about Esau and the generations that became the nation of Edom. There's not much of a spiritual message I can pull out of this, but it again shows God's sovereign design of His-Story, how it all happened. Now there are some questions concerning the names of his wives. (See Genesis 26:34; 28:8–9) You can see there are names that are different from here in Genesis 36:2–3. Why? I don't know. Many have tried to sort this out. Ismael was already dead when Esau took Bashemath for a wife, but there seems there were a father and a son that bedded the same woman who birthed this child that later Esau took for a wife. When we find places like this, after trying unsuccessfully to sort through the possibilities, I just know God knows, and even with these questions unanswered, Esau raised up a family that did become the Nation of Edom, even before Israel ever was.

B. In verses 2 to 8, it explains how it all went down.

1. Of the three wives, Esau had five sons born in Canaan, as well as an unsaid number of daughters.
2. Verses 6 and 7. We see that Esau separated from his father Isaac and his brother Jacob. They were probably on the plains of Mamre (Hebron). The reason was they had such a large herd of livestock that the land was being overgrazed. So, his large herd and all his people left. (Remember he came to meet Jacob with 400 men in Genesis 33:1.) Now, if also we remember Genesis 32:3, Esau ALREADY was in the land of Seir. Edom was already called a country, a nation, and Jake's outfit wasn't in Canaan yet. I think God had already separated Esau from Canaan to prepare Jacob to be transferred over Esau's birthright from Isaac, their father. Esau now has hung his hat in a country called Mount Seir. Seir was a man that had been there in this country, and it seems Esau's family married into Seir's kids and the Nation of Edom was made over the coming years.
3. While this from all recent reports is a very dried-up country, there are a few references bringing me to think it wasn't always so. Verse 37, for instance, talks of a river. Also, if Sodom and Gomorrah were at the south end of the Dead Sea and it was fertile as stated, then not too far away was Edom. Furthermore, I doubt if Esau would have settled in a country that could not support his family's livestock. Also, Edom for a season was a power in the region.

C. As we go through this to keep it simple as possible, verse 9 states Esau became the Nation of Edom around

Mt. Seir, which is south and a little east of the Dead Sea. Then it goes into the generations of his sons from verses 10 to 19. My version calls some of them Dukes, but really, it's easier to understand them as Chiefs of their Clans. Verses 11 and 12 are interesting. Eliphaz had a son by his concubine Timna, who had a son Amelek. The Amalekites were the first bad guys to attack Israel in their wilderness traveling. It seems the place called Rephidim, which was southeast of Mt. Sinai (see Exodus 1:8–16) is where this happened. It was away from Edom, which shows the concubine's son may have been an outcast of the family.

II. The man Seir and his sons.

A. We see back in Genesis 14:6 that these Horites, of whom Seir was their leader, were in this land when Esau moved his family there. Did Esau conquer Seir or just marry into them? (Genesis 3:16) It seems Timna in verse 12 is the same as Timna here in verse 22, so she was older than Esau's son, Eliphaz, which may have been why she was his concubine. But nonetheless, we see in verses 20 to 30 the generations of Seir.

1. Verses 29 and 30 are the names of chieftains of Seir's line. Were these in conjunction with Esau's family? During the time of Moses, I'm sure it was understood better.

III. The Kings of Edom

A. It seems there was no family of one son that stayed in the line of Kings. The new King was from whoever was strongest at the time of the previous King's death. Verse 31 makes it clear Edom was a nation way back before Israel ever was. They will not allow Israel to pass through their land (Numbers 20:14–20) and fought with Israel all through much of Israel's history.

B. Notice in these last verses it seems the King didn't seem to be or go to a certain city to become King and reign but was at the city he was from, and it appears would reign from there. For instance, verse 32, Bela reigned in Edom, and the name of his city was Dinhabah. And verse 35, Hadad whipped the Midianites in Moab, and the name of his city was Avith. So, I count eight Kings mentioned here from verses 31 to 39.

C. Then we see what my version calls Dukes in verses 40 to 43, which again seems to be Chiefs of their Clans; not Kings. To help get this all a little straighter in our minds, those who burned the midnight oil to study this out had to go to traditional writings of Israel to dig a little deeper.

1. The sons of Esau who were said to be Dukes or Chiefs, in verses 15 to 18, these were called Dukes: thirteen in all. These were Chiefs of their clan but not yet rulers of the land of Mt. Seir.
2. Then we see in verse 20 it talks of the Horites (sons of Seir). Go down to verses 29 to 30; these are the Dukes of the Horites that ruled the land but then . . .
3. Verses 31 to 39. Bishop Cumberland (whoever he is) says these Kings were back shortly after (Genesis 14:5–6) the kings of the north came down and whooped on all those little independent kingdoms. The Horites formed an allegiance and had a King who reigned over the area we are studying now before Edom was.
4. Verses 40 to 43. After Edom drove out the Horites it became a REAL Nation. They set up a

nation of Provinces that had Dukes or Chiefs ruling over them, much like Israel in the Book of Judges. This story in Genesis isn't complete enough to get it exactly how it was, but those who research in other books of ancient times came up with this explanation. By and by we'll know the truth when we're Home.

IV. A point of interest.

A. Tradition tells us that when Jake died (Genesis 49; 50) his body was taken as he requested to the cave where his grandpa and father were buried, escorted by Egyptian forces. Well again, by Jewish tradition, Esau came up with a great army and prevented Jake being buried there. But Judah killed Esau (of course he'd be an old, old man by now, easy to kill) and that is how they claimed Esau died. Interesting! Cause in Genesis it doesn't say.

1. Eventually, Edom was raided and conquered by Babylon. Then the Nabateans managed to get into Edom's mountain fortress, Petra, and ran 'um off the mountain to the west; the dry plains called the Negev. Later, the Jews in the Maccabee's time whooped on them, and they killed many; those they didn't convert to the Jewish religion and now are no more.

Apart from God, the world cannot stand. All these things were foretold by God's prophets. Obadiah would be good to read concerning Edom's destruction. Well, no more is said about Jake's twin until Romans 9:10–18.

Blessings, to ya all, Mike

<u>Questions for Discussion</u>

1. Does God love all individuals? (Romans 9:13,18)
2. Also, John 3:16 ". . . loves the world" is pointing to the fact of all Creation. Humanity is the apple of God's eye; however, knowing the fall of man will come. His decree is in verses 13,18. His wish is seen in 1 Timothy 2:4; His feelings. Yet, in His righteous purpose, His decree stands. (Romans 9:10–24) Understanding the word Decree would be very helpful to you. Most Christians don't like to deal with this truth. They cling to the idea that God loves all and gives us a choice which does not hold water with Scripture. Keep 1 Corinthians 2:14 and Romans 8:7 in mind.

Jacob Loves Joseph More than His Other Sons; Causes Jealousy and Hate, yet Joseph Follows God

Hi, folks. Got through Esau's chapter. Now we're studying a guy who God blessed, and in my view, a type of Christ. Not only did he seem to be walking with God his whole life through terrible trials, but God used him to save Israel when he was made second in command under the Pharaoh in Egypt. An interesting story.

Let's pray.

Genesis 37:1–36 KJV

I. Jacob is in the country of his birth, the "Promised Land." His boys are men.

A. Verses 1 and 2. Seems this is going on before Isaac's death. Joe is seventeen. He was born in Paddan-Aram about six years before they left there to come back here to Canaan. So, if he's seventeen, it's been about eleven years since they left Laban. All but Benny, (he's one or two) are in their twenties and thirties; men if you will. Not necessarily upstanding men. They remind me some of Cain and Able. They have what the world calls "anger management" issues. Some have proven they are killers.

    1. In verse 2, Joe was out herding sheep with his four brothers from the two concubines. They

were doing something wrong, but it doesn't say what, so we can't assume what direction of evil it was, although it seems to be bad more than a little. There are those who say he was a tattle-tale, but quite possibly this was something that had to be dealt with. As we'll see, Ol' Joe is a very wise for his age guy. He's also a pretty good organizer, and he's dependable. (These are, of course, from God for God's purpose.)

B. Verse 3. Herein is the big mistake Jake made concerning his fatherhood. He loves Joe more than the rest. This, of course, is selfish love and hurts the other boys. Naturally, they are jealous. Then, to top it off, Jake openly declares his love above the rest by giving Joe a long-sleeved, bathrobe type of coat made with many colors. This is a sign of superiority. Now that really stirs up the flames of jealousy. Verse 4, remember 1 John 3:15?

1. Verses 5 to 11. It doesn't say God spoke to Joseph in a dream, but obviously, it was God for what he dreams did come to pass. All this is according to God's providence (remember it means prearrangement). God has a plan as he explained it to Abraham in Genesis 15:13, and this will be the way it will play out.

   a. Both dreams basically tell the brothers that Joe is going to be their Sovereign someday. They will bow down before him as God planned. This will get the fire of hate really burning! Then in the second dream, He also tells his father. Of course, the sun and the moon are Ma and Pa, and the eleven stars are his brothers. Here Jake has some discernment and begins to think maybe God might be behind this. Verse 11.

II. James 1:15 is in their hearts; hatred begins.

A. Without any thought of God, or God's purpose, in the heart of these brothers was conceived lust, jealousy, hatred, and then the completion – murder. This story portrays James 1:15 very well; no thought of God, only self. I'm not completely sold on the assumption that Joe was being self-righteous in telling this any more than God was, having this truth known knowing the end result will be Joseph will be in Egypt as God intends to be. As we'll see, Joe seems to be trusting God through all that happens to him and is blessed.

1. Verses 12 to 17. This story starts out with Jake giving Joe the mission to see how his boys are caring for the folk's herds. This is more than a fifty-mile walk he's sending this 17-year-old boy on. Herds have to move, so it's a general idea of somewhere in the Shechem country are your brothers. See how they're fairing with our livestock and report back to me. It seems he's going alone. Gets to Shechem country probably the second day, sees a man (verse 15) who tells him where to find his brothers, at Dothan. That is about 15-miles north of Shechem with a roundabout trail perhaps 20 miles. So off he goes again. Now the story gets bad.

B. Verses 18 to 22. They saw him coming from afar off, meaning it was an open country and him walking. They start planning to kill him.

1. Notice they say, "then let's see if his dreams come to be." They're thinking just like Satan concerning God's promise of the "Seed of the Woman," all his attempts to stop that Seed from being. Of course, it failed for as nothing can stop what God has purposed (Isaiah.14:24) therefore, likewise, these brothers are trying to stop what they can't. Also, they're sending him on the mission God intended. But I'm getting ahead of His-Story. They think we'll just kill him then throw him in a hole. When the rains come, he'll be gone. But Ruben, the oldest, says no, just put him in a pit alive and let him die without us shedding his blood. Notice he's not as violent as his brothers. He plans to sneak back there later and take Joseph to their father.

III. God's purpose to send Joseph to Egypt begins.

A. Verses 23 to 25. So, Joseph comes to them, and they grab ahold of him, tear off his coat of superiority over them, then throw him in this pit, a dry well. I'm sure Joe wasn't quiet, probably begging his brothers not to do this thing. But they do. Then they sit down to eat! Reuben must have left, verse 29, for he seems to be gone when the next thing happens.

1. Verses 25 to 28. Judah sees a way to make a profit out of this deal and not be guilty of murder. They were on a trade route to Egypt, and some Ishmeelites and Midianites were passing by. The thought came to Judah, sell the Brat! Make a buck or two off him! So, he talks his brothers into it. When some Ishmeelites again come near, the brothers strike up a bargain and make twenty pieces of silver off him (the price of a full-grown

slave was about thirty pieces of silver). The evil deed is done, but it was falling right into God's purpose!

2. Ruben returns and sees the brothers are gone. He looks into the dry well and sees Joe's gone too. He hurries after his brothers and asks what happened to little Joe? They spell it out for him, just what went down (probably proud of themselves). But Ruben is terribly distressed and did what people did back then, tore his perfectly good shirt to show how bad he felt.

3. Jump to verse 36, and we'll get to Jake last. Here it says the Midianites (several places they used Ishmeelites and Midianites interchanged, why I don't know, see Judges 8:24–26) sold poor Joey to a guy by the name of Potiphar. This guy was a married eunuch. (That had to be tuff on his wife since they couldn't have sex. Many I've heard are castrated which might explain his wife's actions with little Joey, but more on that later.) He was "Captain of the Guards," in charge of killing the condemned. The Hebrew word in this case for "officer" is saris, which has the meaning of eunuch. Guards really mean the Executioners. So, that's where Joseph ends up for now in Egypt. He'll stay with Potiphar through the next chapter while we take a closer look at Judah's dysfunctional family.

B. Back to Jacob, verses 31 to 35. The brothers decide on a good lie to get themselves out of trouble with their dad. They kill a goat, bloody Joe's coat (probably tear it too) and then ask their father if this was Joe's coat. Of course, Jake knew it was. They said it appears Joe was eaten since the coat was found lying on the ground by itself.

1. Verse 34. Jacob mourns to the point of near death; his heart is broken. Like when anyone mourns, God comforting him is not thought of, he's grieving like a man with no Hope like those without God.

2. Verse 35. His sons, the hypocrites they are, try to comfort him. Now here we see apparently Jake had more daughters than just Dinah since it says, daughters. But their comforting is to no avail. He's actin' like he's totally forgotten God and how God has protected him and provided for him. He's just like one of those born only once, without hope in God. This is the condition we leave Jake in till the end of Genesis. Now we will look at that rascal Judah and then focus back on Joseph for basically the rest of this book.

Have a good week! We had a blessed time with family in Alaska last weekend. Izzy did a great performance in the play he was acting in. He was the lead role, and there was a good message in the play for Alaskan natives. However, it was a secular play, so pointing Christ for truth wasn't there. But it showed the mess that is there, and in this case, something good came out.

Blessings, Mike

Question for Discussion

1. Faith to match your circumstances. Here we see a broken heart that causes one to forget God is there and act like one with no hope. I don't know what I'd be like if that happened to me. Do you honestly know how you would handle it? 1 Corinthians 10:12 points me to realize by grace

we stand. What did Jesus say in John 15:5? So, what should we acknowledge, and what should we ask for?

The Beginning of the Tribe of Judah from Whom Our Lord and Savior Came

Mornin' folks. We got through the selling of brother Joey into slavery as God intended to get him to Egypt. Now we come to Judah, fourth down from the top of Jake's sons and it seems he separates himself from his family at this time. Let's see if we can figure out what's goin' on.

Let's pray.

Genesis 38:1–30 KJV

I. The shameful act of selling his brother may have led him to withdraw from his brothers.

A. Now, in verse 1, it says Judah, "went down from his brethren." In other words, he pulled out from his family. Why? It doesn't say but let's give him the benefit of the doubt and assume he felt rotten, which well he should. He sees the pain he caused his father and, as often times, if God gives us some conscience of right and wrong, guilt comes after the deed is done. Being around home makes him feel bad so gets his servants to round up his stock, packs his camels, and starts lookin' for new ground to begin again.

1. Let's figure out ages here. Seems Joe was seventeen, so that would put Judah at about twenty-seven. Later it says in Genesis 41:46, Joe was thirty when he stood before the Pharaoh. Then we'll see there are seven years of good crops, then there will be seven years of drought. Two years into the drought Jacob's boys go down to Egypt to get some grain. So, from the time little Joe is taken to Egypt to when the brothers go down is twenty-two years (give or take a few), just so we can see the time frame.

II. Judah's family begins but is not pleasing to God.

A. Verses 2 to 11. So, he wanders northwest 15-miles near the village of Adullam and seems to be befriended by one of the locals named Hirah. Now as his servants were tending his flocks, he got to wander around and see the sights. One of the sights he really liked was a Canaanite girl whose father was Shuah. Seems this wasn't an arranged marriage but probably took her and shacked-up; not for sure but seems so. Right away, and one right after another, she gave Judah three sons. Er, meaning Watcher, then Onan, meaning Strong, and then little Shelah. I'm not sure what his name means. Notice the first son Judah names, then his common-law wife names the second one. Interesting seems she may have named Shelah too. As we know, the Canaanites weren't on the top of God's list as good people. They earned that rep cuz they were a lustful, rebellious people without fear of the God of Noah. Perhaps these boys were influenced by their mother's side of the family. Whatever the case, time went on, probably eighteen years give or take a couple, and Judah decided it's time to find a proper wife for his oldest son. He found one he thought was just right and presented her to Er. Well, it doesn't say if Er disliked

Tamar or not, but what it was, it was pure evil that Er did in the sight of the Lord. (He sees everything anyway.) God killed him dead! Verse 7.

1. Now, back then, they had customs that directed the families. This was a contracted marriage and Judah was obligated to see that Tamar was cared for, as well as he needed her to have a son. In the case of this happening, the next son in line is to take the wife of the dead elder son and raise their son as the heir of the eldest son. Both these sons were rebellious; probably their mother was too. (Judah likely married her for the wrong reason. Lust may have led him to her, which is often the case.) So here in verse 9, we see Onan would not obey his father's command. While he still had sex with Tamar, he pulled out of her; spilled the beans on the floor. Verse10. That again brought on the wrath of God and He killed Onan dead too! I'm sure Judah at this point is thinking, "if this is God doing this, we've got trouble!"

2. Verse 11. Shelah is somewhere about thirteen to fifteen-years-old, and Judah tells Tamar to wait a few years, don't marry anyone you can have my youngest son in a couple of years.

III. Judah's wife dies, and he forgets his word to Tamar.

A. Verses 12 to 23. It's too joined together to break this up as the whole story flows through these fourteen verses.

1. First, his wife dies. Not sure if it's right after Onan dies, but as soon then as the year of mourning passes. Judah has ignored Tamar and the fact

that Shelah is of age to take on a wife, and Tamar knows.

2. Now it is sheep-shearing time, so it's party time in the little town of Timnath. Judah's buddy Hirah probably talks Judah into it. "Let's get you up there and get your mind off of the past and party!" So, they go.

3. Verse 14. Tamar hears of Judah's plans and says to herself, "Judah's not getting out of the contract!" She knows what Judah's mainly going up there for and she gets herself ready and puts on the big skedaddle and gets to the gate of the town before Judah does. She shows herself as a whore which Judah was going for anyway. He sees her and likes what he sees, so tells her to go and get ready for him. Verse 16. Well, Tamar is a pretty sharp gal and says, "What will you give me?" Verse 17. Judah tells her the kid of a goat. Ok, she says but ya got to give now something to guarantee the deal. Verse 18. It's agreed his seal or the stamp he wears on a cord tied on his neck and his staff. At the time when he'd send the kid, she'd give back the seal and staff. Well, the deed was done as planned out by Tamar, but also by God (Proverbs 16:9). She got pregnant. Then she went home and put on her widow outfit again. Verse 19.

4. Here in verses 20 to 23, Judah sent his promised kid of a goat but Hirah, whom he sent, couldn't find her. In fact, in Timnath, there were no whores now. These gals were of the type who were, at that time, part of their religion. Apparently, there wasn't any temple there, so there really weren't any whores around town. Then when his buddy Hiram comes back and tells Judah there's no such woman to be found, he

drops the whole thing. Basically says, "I tried to pay her, but she's not in town. She can have the pledge, for whatever that is worth to her." Truth is, it will save her life and convict Judah of his wrong to her! I don't understand, but it sure seems there was some shame on Judah's part. As immoral as the Canaanites were, why this would cause shame, I don't know, but it did. (God, through Jacob, did probably raise Judah to marry first and stay with only her, but I'm guessing.) So, he dropped the whole thing and let it go. Three months' time passed. Then some rumors started to spread about Tamar.

IV. Tamar gets her satisfaction from Judah's word, and Judah sees his wrong.

A. Verses 24 to 26. Somebody tells Judah his daughter-in-law played the whore and is pregnant. This hurt his pride. (Also, she was to be Shelah's wife even though Judah is hoping she forgets the deal.) Apparently back then, like now with those evil Muslims, they could kill women without any thought that it takes two to get a woman pregnant. Just the woman would be punished, not the man. Well, sir, Judah goes after her, and she is (I'm thinkin' she's cool and calm knowing what's gonna happen) brought forth but she has some evidence to protect her. Seems she's now in front of Judah and shows the Stamp and Staff and says, (I like this lady's style) "whom this belongs to is the Joker who got me pregnant." Well sir, what else could he say? The stamp was known to be his, and I'm bettin' back then a staff was also marked so known to whom it belongs. Judah knows he's been had and he's guilty as charged!

1. Now comes the question. Which part of 2 Corinthians 7:10 is happening to Judah? Is this Godly sorrow and true repentance or does he see he's been caught? He says, "I see she is more righteous than me." In our English translations, there are two thoughts of what Judah did with concern to Tamar. It seems he left her alone from then on and appeared never to marry again. From these three sons (as well see Tamar gave Judah twins) started the growth of the tribe of Judah. However, there is in Hebrews a translation that the phrase really means he never stopped seeing her. In other words, he kept her in his house, and they raised the boys from her. (I'm kind of a romantic, so I hope it's the Hebrews translation.) Fact is, we don't know which.

B. It's TWINS! and they're boys! Verses 28 to 30. You can read these verses, and you'll see it's much like the birth of Jacob and Esau. The one twin they named Zarah, stuck his hand out and they tied a string to it. Then he withdrew it (probably testing to see if it was too cold or not). Anyway, just like Esau did, Pharez came out first. But here there is a difference, for this time the firstborn will be the Chosen "Seed of the Woman" transporter. You can find him in our Lord's genealogy in Luke 3:23–38. In verse 33, it's spelled, Phares.

All this was God's doing. This was His authorship of His-Story, an amazing turn of events! Why this way? Why not! It's His-Story! But it's interesting He interrupts the story of Joseph here to show the key tribe of Israel, Judah, who not only will King David be from, but then the Lion of Judah, our Lord. They will be separated from the rest of Israel and stand alone for a long time. Just like Judah is doing here. After Israel and Judah split up, Israel had NO Godly kings and eventually was taken out for good. Yet, God blessed the tribe of Judah by raising up, from time to time, Godly Kings who followed Him (at least part of the time). While they did rebel and were driven out for seventy years, God told them they'd come back. They did and were a country till after our Lord went to the Cross and rose again. Later they were cast out by the Romans.

Well, next week, we'll catch up to Joe in Egypt.

Blessings, to ya all, Mike

Back to Joseph in Potiphar's House; God's Got It All Planned Out!

Well, good mornin' folks. We got to look at the start of "The Lion of Judah's" tribe, that will become our Lord and Savior. Now we're back to Joseph. He's a slave in the house of Potiphar. I guess I'll explain the politics of that Dynasty in Egypt. It's important to understand this as to why things went so well for Jacob's family when he first came to Egypt.

So, before this happened to little Joe, there were some half-breed Shemetics who were more advanced in bronze-made weapons, as well as military tactics, and had incorporated the use of horse-drawn chariots to fight with. Their name was Hyksos. There seemed to be a drought that pushed them to move west across the Sinai Peninsula. They invaded Egypt. The Egyptian Dynasty of that time could not stop the Hyksos on their chariots and were whooped on. Hyksos took over. However, these guys were smart and allowed everyone to basically live and let live, and ruled well, and Egypt prospered and was at peace most of their reign.

Later they were ousted by the next Dynasty to be, who were again Egyptians. Now, this helps (God's providence) set the stage for what God planned. Firstly, the Hyksos were friendly to their relatives the Hebrews, and so, it wasn't too hard to see Joseph rising to be second in command of Egypt. Secondly, when the next dynasty came to power, they treated the Hebrews poorly and made them slaves. So, now the stage is set. Let's take a look at Joe's life in particular.

Let's pray.

Genesis 39:1–23 KJV

A. Verse 1 just tells us again what we learned in chapter 37, as a slave Joe was sold to this high-ranking officer of Egypt, Potiphar. He was in charge of punishments for crimes against the Pharaoh. He was a Eunuch which usually means one is castrated so as not to interfere with one's committed duties, but possibly not here. Most likely the term just means High-Court Official. So be that as it may, Joe is in his house to serve him.

B. Verses 2 and 3 state clearly, "The Lord was with him." We see he had a faith that seemed to make him realize this: when the world gives you lemons, make lemonade. He is knowing and trusting God, who has His reasons for these hard times. He doesn't seem to get bitter and feel sorry for himself but jumps right into what God dished out to him and does real good. To have God with oneself, you will recognize that, as well as others, for this is Faith in knowing God has a purpose even when you don't understand the suffering one is going through. I'm sure Jacob has told Joseph about God's promise concerning their family, as well as the promise of the "Seed of the Woman" concerning the savior to come. For all this, God gave Joseph a strong dose of faith. I'll always be wondering how much understanding Joe had concerning what was told to grandpa Abe back in Genesis 15:13 and when did he understand what he said to his brothers in Genesis 50:20 (read those and try to see what I'm getting at). For he seems to not fall apart, no matter how bad it gets. Yes, they may not have mentioned it, and it did perhaps get him depressed, but if so, it doesn't seem to show. For he's industrious, wise for his age, and honest, as well as faithful to whom he serves.

1. In verses 4 and 5, we see Potiphar realized Joe could be trusted to the point he gave Joe complete control of his household affairs. Verse 6. This is amazing, considering what his brothers did to him, how he is still holding it together. It is an amazing Faith that Joe has, and his character stood out to where a heathen recognized the true God in Joseph. Verse 3.

II. Here comes trouble from bad to worse, yet still he is blessed by God.

A. Now, here again, God proves the character of this young man. Verses 7 to 9. Joe is doing 2 Timothy 2:22. While this is a command to those who are in Christ, Joseph is in Christ, for he is trusting in the Promises of God. Therefore, with the power of God in him, Joe was able to stand against sin and the wiles of the Devil. Where some who are in Christ may fall, he didn't. These commands are then our responsibility to obey and bring glory to God. The grace to stand can only come from God. (1 Corinthians 7:7 Paul could go anywhere and not be tempted to lust after women. Not many men are given this gift, but here we see Joseph did have this gift, and it is a gift!) This would be tuff on most Christian men, but the proof of who Joseph is serving is in his statement in verse 9, "how can I do this great wickedness and SIN against God!" Amazing! The faith this young man had in his God! God is obviously at the forefront of his mind! I truthfully cannot say that of myself. As I recently read

Job 19, verses 1 to 22, how he was not only devastated by the loss of his children and the loss of all he had and the pain in his body he suffered, but his friends and all were blaming him for what happened to him. He saw that it was God who persecuted him. He then wished all this about him would be written down in stone for every generation to see. Verses 23 and 24. Then daylight appeared in his memory. Verses 25 to 27. He remembered God's promise of his redemption when this life is over. He will be free of this sorrow. But here with this story, that is revealed to us, at least what is written, he never despairs to the depth of Job. God's hand of grace was continually on him and the Devil never had his way. While this young man in this story doesn't seem to sin, I'm sure he did. But as Christ withstood temptation it seems, at least what is written, Joseph served God, and God uses him to save Israel.

1. So, Potiphar's wife didn't have her way with him. This doesn't mean Joe didn't fornicate with other women, but it doesn't say anything such as that, so I'll assume he didn't. The main thing here is, while he wouldn't sin against God with her, he was also faithful to his master just like it says to be in Ephesians 6:5–8. Amazing to me, and I feel guilty knowing I have not always been so! Thank God for his mercy and the promise in Romans 8:1.
2. Verse 10. She was still after Joe to commit adultery DAY AFTER DAY, yet he didn't give in!
3. Verses 11 to 13. Then it happened. She was lusting so bad for him, she grabbed him, and when Joe pulled away, the outer garment he was wearing came off, and he ran from her. Then in verses 14 and 15, she was now mad at Joe for not having sex with her. She called in more servants

and said, "that Hebrew of Potiphar's tried to rape me!"

4. Verses 16 to 18. When Potiphar came home, she lied to him and said Joe attempted to rape her.

III. I'm in the dog house now! Only I'm innocent! I've been framed!

A. Verses 19 and 20. Potiphar was Hot! But instead of killing Joe in some way, remember Potiphar was in charge of the punishment that was done to those who committed a crime against the Pharaoh so he could have easily had him killed, after all a slave was no different than a dog or horse to the owner, yet instead he had them throw Joe into the prison that he was the boss of.

B. Verses 21 to 23. But this was how God intended this to go down and again it says God was with Joseph. Somehow perhaps Potiphar told his master of the prison how good Joe was managing his household and could be trusted, but whatever it was, God again showed mercy to little Joey, and the prison boss turned over the prisoners' work list to Joe, and he was the little boss of the prison. Things went well and were better than ever before. The prison boss could go on vacation and was confident that the prison would be run well by little Joey who was now perhaps twenty, maybe twenty-three, who knows, but a young guy.

A thought to consider: so, now we come to the end of the chapter, and the thing we can pull out for our good is the example of faith in God that one of His Born-Again children should have in one's Heavenly father. This has been a good lesson for me to bring this truth to my remembrance. Something came up a short time ago, and little Joey's faith came to mind. I was able to peacefully say, "OK, this is what God wants. He will provide!" And I had Peace over the whole thing. Thank You, Lord! Hope it'll help you all.

Blessings, Mike

God is Going to Exalt Joseph a Little Later; Meanwhile, Joseph Interprets a Couple Dreams

Mornin' folks. We had a real warm day yesterday, and not much wind looks like the last taste of summer. It was a cool fall up to then; yesterday was 80 above. Now it's 52 and windy. Gonna rain today, then get cooler as the week progresses. It is fall. Beautiful colors; leaves are red, yellow, and gold. The pines and spruce are always green, so good mix. The Lord is the greatest Artist! We left Joseph in prison but seems he's again in a position of responsibility. Let's see what God's plans are for him.

Let's pray.

Genesis 40:1–23 KJV

I. Some trouble in the Pharaoh's court. The butler and the baker end up in the slammer (prison) where Joe is.

  A. Let's stop and reflect on God's timing with Joe.

    1. He showed to his father he was trustworthy. Jake was partial to him over the other sons, yet appeared to be led by God.

    2. Then in Potiphar's house, Joseph again proved responsible and was put in complete control of the household affairs. He's again handed a bag

of sour lemons in life and winds up in Potiphar's prison. Instead of getting depressed, he proves his worth again and is put in charge of the prison's inward affairs.

3. Now some think he was arrogant and had to be disciplined and humbled. I'm not sure that's so. It's more likely God's timing for His plan to be carried out. Joe will be thirty-years-old when he's placed in charge of Egypt's grain storage project. David became King at age thirty. God proved that He was with them both before they were placed in power. The key I think is the proof God WAS with them, and those around them knew He WAS with them. They both over and over showed faith in the Most-High God as they went through their dark valleys, trusting God. Remember David in killing Goliath? (1 Samuel 17:26; 17:45) Likewise, shortly we'll see Joseph says only God can interpret dreams, tell me. Verse 8. Meaning he knows God is with him and using him for a purpose. How much Joseph knows at this time (Genesis 37:5–11) I can't say, but may well trust the previous dream he had where his family will all bow down before him knowing what God says will be. (I'm speculating.)

B. Verse 4. We see the Captain of the Guard put Joe in charge of them: close contact. Then in verses 5 and 6, we see God gave them dreams that confused them and worried them. (They were both sad; worried for their lives.)

1. At this point, we start to see God's plan develop, verses 7 and 8, being he asked them, "what's up?" They told him of the dreams they couldn't under-

stand. Here we see it's clear Joseph knows he is God's servant and is able to interpret dreams. "Do not interpretations belong to God? Tell me them, I ask you." Well, Joe knows God will voice the interpretations through him. This tells us Joe is in tune with God, and he knows it just like Elijah knew it.

C. Verses 9 to 19. They tell him, and Joe tells them what's gonna happen to them.

1. The butler is going to be brought out of jail, and he's going to serve Pharaoh at his birthday party. Joe tells him this, but really God has revealed this to Joseph; he's God's prophet.

2. Now the timing is still not right for Joe to be placed in his role as prime minister (second to Pharaoh, so we'll call him this). He'll have to wait two more years. As we'll see, God has His reasons and His timing when He makes His moves, and it's always just the right time. Right? But Joe, in verse 16 asks the butler to remember him when he gets back to work for the Pharaoh. He explains he's innocent. But God won't remind the butler about the young man in prison who interprets dreams till the Pharaoh dreams a strange dream no one can interpret which is God's plan.

3. Then we come to the baker, verses 16 to 19. The butler's dream went well, so he thought he'd try his luck. (Luck is forgetting God in our lives and thinking it's all by chance.) He told Joe his dream. In his case, it's in three days as well, but the birds eating his bread is to signify that birds will eat his dead carcass hung on a tree. His appointed time to die is close at hand; then he'll step into eternity.

(Hebrews 9:27) Hell awaits him sad thing, a fearful thing.

II. The Pharaoh's birthday party is on, and Joseph was correct.

A. Verses 20 to 23. What God says will be! Good old Isaiah 14:24. Ya just can't get away from that verse! Everything goes down as Joseph prophesied. It was from God.

1. Verse 23. It wasn't time for Joe to get free. God will stir the butler's memory in a couple years, but first God will give the Pharaoh a serious dream that no one on his religious staff can understand. Then the stage will be set for Joseph to enter the King's Court. All in God's timing!

Joseph is about to be put on a throne, and the prophesy of others bowing down to him is at hand! Have a great weekend.

God Bless you all! Mike

Question for Discussion

1. This study – is it a good example that God is orchestrating His-Story according to His Will? How does this stack up to those who believe in what they say, "God has given man free will?" Dig a little on this question. I mean search the Bible Scriptures – not rely on your reasoning. The Bible must support your answer. Psalms 139:1–16 may help. Verse 16 is the summary and Proverbs 16:9.

From Rags to Riches or Up from the Prison He Arose!

Mornin' folks. I see, looking out our window over the Lake that the sun has risen and is shining out through the clouds. Reminds me that the SON has risen also and my hope is confident for He's Alive! In this study, God is showing us what His purpose for Joseph going through all these hard times was about. It seems Joe trusted God through it all which amazes me. So, let's get to studying.

Let's pray.

Genesis 41:1–57 KJV

I. Two full years have passed, and the Pharaoh has a troubling Dream

A. Verse 1. As we saw, the butler was back with the Pharaoh but didn't try to help Joe out of prison. That's because God's timing wasn't at hand. Now it is the time to place Joseph before the King.

B. Verses 2 to 8 explain the dream. The number seven comes up throughout this. That's the number favored by God. It often represents perfection. Notice also; God uses two examples of what's going down; fat cows and starving cows, then ears of grain full and heavy, and ears of grain empty and dry. What does it mean? Pharaoh is troubled; he's sure it's a warning for the starving ate the fat ones. He manages to sleep again but then had the dream this time with the grain. What does this mean? He calls his witchcraft people, and those who seem smarter than the average person, but no one can explain the dreams.

II. Then the butler; God jogs his memory about the young man in prison who told what his dream meant.

A. Verses 9 to13 are pretty clear and recount what happened in prison concerning his and the baker's dreams, and that Joseph interpreted them exactly as to what happened. This excited Pharaoh for he was troubled a lot over this dream.

B. Verses 14 to 24. Pharaoh wasted no time getting Joe out of prison. Verse 14 says Joe had to clean up before he could go before the Pharaoh. Doesn't say, but I'm sure they gave him clothes to wear as well as shaved his head.

1. In verses 15 and 16, the Pharaoh questions Joe about his ability to interpret dreams, and Joseph gives credit where credit is due. I'm thinkin' of Proverbs 3:6 right now. This is what a servant of God should and/or will do. He points out that only God can do this. Therefore Joe is declaring he is a servant of the Most-High God!
   a. So, the Pharaoh tells him what we already read verses 17 to 24.

III. Joseph explains the dream and sets the stage for Israel to come to Egypt.

A. Verses 25 to 32. First off, Joseph states the reason God gave this dream to Pharaoh is that it's gonna happen right quick! You'd best prepare! Now Pharaoh doesn't know the true God of Heaven and Earth. But he's about to know of Him, for what Joseph tells him comes to pass.

1. So, there's gonna be seven years of abundant harvests, that's the fat cows and full heavy ears of grain. Right? Then will come "starvin' times," seven years also. We need to pay attention to verse 32; the double dream is to get their attention! It's gonna come down real soon and real hard; people will starve! So, what ya gonna do? Here comes God's advice through the man of God, Joseph.

B. Verses 33 to 38. God tells Pharaoh what to do step by step through Joseph.

1. Appoint a wise man who knows how to organize. Verse 33. (Know that's gonna be Joe.)
2. Verse 34. He then appoints officers that will make sure one-fifth part of all farmland will be harvested and stored away for the starvin' times.
3. Verse 35. Each city will have storage facilities for the surplus harvest.
4. Verse 36. Each of the one-fifth of the harvest for the seven years will not be touched to ensure enough food will be at hand for the seven years of drought. (That's a long-time dry spell!)

IV. Guess who the Pharaoh appoints as the wise man over the grain storage? God's directing here as always!

A. Verses 37 to 45. The Pharaoh (directed by God) lays out what Joseph will do and his authority to do it.

1. Notice in verse 38 Pharaoh states he recognizes God is directing Joseph. It's interesting to me that Pharaoh proclaims – God IS! Which means

he knows there is THE God! Again, I'm thinkin' of a New Testament verse Romans 1:18–23, "All of mankind." (I never thought of man as Kind. You? Of course, "kind" means the kind of critter we are.) Nonetheless, these verses are the way we ALL are till God Elects us. Pretty soon, Joe is going to be Egyptianized in appearance. But we'll see he doesn't lose his faith in the true God.

2. So, he gives Joe his ring, which signifies Joe's Pharaoh-given authority. Verse 42. Then Pharaoh had a parade made in Joe's honor for all to recognize Joseph as who we'll call the Prime Minister of Egypt. Only the Pharaoh will be above Joseph. No one can do anything but by Joe's say so. Verse 43. "Ruler over ALL of Egypt." This is where God intended Joseph to be; He raised Joe up for this very thing! As he does all people for what purpose God intends no matter how small or how great. (Psalms 139:16 and Isaiah 14:24–27) All this before He created the Heavens and the Earth! This IS His-Story! Also, Romans 9:17, "I raised Pharaoh up" (a different Pharaoh). This is an excellent example that it's God who worketh all things after the counsel of His OWN will. (Ephesians 1:11) The point we often forget before anything else, everything, and I mean everything, is ALL for the Glory of God! Amen!

3. Notice in verse 43, "Bow the Knee." Remember the prophecy Joseph spoke in Genesis 37:9? His brothers will bow to Joseph!

4. Verse 45. Pharaoh gives Joe the Egyptian name "Zaphnath-paaneah." Then he gives him a wife who is the daughter of the top witch doctor. "On" is where they went to really worship "RA," the Egyptian Sun God.

V. Joseph gets to work both for Egypt and making a family.

A. Verses 46 to 57. Notice here in verse 46, Joe is thirty, so from seventeen-years-old to thirty – thirteen years a slave! He held onto his faith throughout that time! So, it continues exactly as God said through Joseph. Seven years of great harvest came, and Joe had it stored in the many cities of Egypt. They were rich, just like God intended them to be. Skip down to verses 54 to 57. The seven years of good and plenty ended, then the bad years came in verse 55. The Pharaoh commanded all people to go to Joseph for food, and being God warned the Pharaoh of what was coming, Egypt had a surplus to sell the rest of the world or better the neighboring countries. Verse 57 sets the stage for Israel to come and see Joseph.

B. Meanwhile, Joe in his free time started a family and had two sons, Manasseh, whose name means "the one who causes me to forget" (forget all the trials he's gone through) and Ephraim whose name means "fruitful" (this will be the largest tribe of Israel). By the way, these are Hebrew names, not Egyptian. Here is a perfect example of how often times God set things in motion according to His purpose, while we wonder just what's going on! We often forget God is in control of His artistically crafted STORY. He's truly the Greatest Author Ever! Well, we'll see next that Joe's brothers will bow down before the little, brat brother they hated! But we'll also see "The Man of God" (Joseph) displaying righteous understanding.

We're up in Alaska now with our daughter. She's in the process of moving so we'll see how much studying I get done.

Blessings, To ya All! Mike

Question for Discussion

1. What I'm hoping you readers begin to see clearly is that "Life" is God's story, and His-Story is crafted dramatically like no other. For all other stories written are a part of His-Story, as well as YOU are a part of His-Story. Do ya see that? I never cease to be amazed at God's craftsmanship and His artistic design of all things.

The Start of the Prophecy of Genesis 15:13 God has His Reasons not Necessarily Understood by Us

Mornin' folks. Writing to ya all from up North in Fairbanks, Alaska. It's not cold yet, only right now 31 degrees above Fahrenheit or -1 Celsius. It's been a little colder but not much. Well, we've seen Joseph finally get where God intended him to be as second in command of all Egypt. Now the seven good years are over, and we start up the second year of starvin' times. God's sending Jacob's ten rascals down to Egypt now to buy grain.

Let's pray.

Genesis 42:1–24 KJV

I. Genesis 41:57 says, "All nations came to Egypt to buy grain," and here Jacob hears of grain there for sale.

A. Verses 1 and 2. Jake says it straight out, quit acting like you don't know what to do! Take the mule train down to Egypt and buy grain. We are almost out of grub! If this is in the second year of drought, their livestock is dying, which gives me pause to wonder just how many of their herds and flocks are still alive by the time they move to Egypt?

1. Verses 3 to 6. So, they run into starvin' times in Canaan. They didn't have planes or container

ships so if one didn't want to starve ya had to move on your own.

> a. Say there were 500 people attached to Jakes outfit, think of the number of mules they had to have to bring enough back to do any good. Plus, they had to have a travelin' outfit too, so we're talkin' 100 mules or more, not just ten. They had to have pack saddles, halters, panyardbags (pack bags), etc. Lash ropes too. 200 pounds a mule times 100 = 20,000 lbs. How long would that last them? Say 4 pounds per person a day times 500 people = 2,000 lbs. a day they'd eat. (A person may not eat 4 lbs. a day, but milk goats gotta be figured into that as well!) So, maybe it would last 10 days! They're gonna need more than 100 mules to get through a month!

2. Verse 6. The prophecy of Genesis 37:9 comes to pass. They are bowed down in front of their little brother! But they don't know it yet.

II. How Joseph deals with his brothers.

A. Verses 7 to 20. Joe's about thirty-nine or so now, he's been blessed by God with wisdom. He knew his family eventually will have to come cause of the drought and because of the prophecy to his great-grandfather, Abe, in Genesis 15:13. Now he sees them, but they don't know him.

1. Verse 9. Joe decides to work their fear toward him to search out the truth concerning his little brother, Benny. They don't know he speaks their language so when an interpreter isn't around;

they're talking openly. Now, it's possible they also speak a Canaan dialect that is their "trade" language. There's probably not too many who know Hebrew; their numbers are few and they are not a nation yet.

2. So, he says straight out, I think you're spies! That puts the fear in them!

   a. They try to talk their way out but Joe's having none of it. They see they're at this Egyptian's mercy and it looks like he's not giving them any. They're up against a river with rapids a'comin' fast at 'um, and they have no paddle! They fear they're between a rock and a hard spot. They call themselves "true men" meaning they are honest men of good character (which we know is a lie; they're first-class rascals!). They don't persuade Joe and he calls them spies.

   b. He tells them what's going to be, verse 16. Send one of your brothers and bring that little brother of yours back, then I'll let ya go and give you grain. Joe sends them to the slammer for three days to let them sweat it out, but brings them out and lays out what he really is going to have them do. Verse 18. "I fear God." Here they hear him say he looks to the same God their fathers do in faith. (I'm sure they're surprised.) Then verses 19 and 20 lay out what he really intended for them. Just one brother will stay in prison; the rest go back with the grain so their families won't starve. Bring back your little brother, and you'll not die. They agreed.

B. Verses 21 to 24. Now they confess amongst themselves. They say they are being punished for their crime cause of what they did to their little brother Joey, their own blood brother. Reuben is especially angry with them and himself for this happening to them. "And his blood shall be required," meaning they know we're gonna get it now! This is punishment from God!

1. Verses 23 and 24. Joe grieves here at hearing their acknowledgment of their terrible sin remembering the fear and pain they put him through, but he loves them yet, which only one by God's grace could do.
2. He comes back and finishes his instructions to them. Simeon, who was the bloodiest of them all, would be held in chains in prison. He, if you remember, instigated and followed through with killing off all the males in Shechem with Levi, then was trying to kill Joseph outright but was stopped by Reuben and Judah. So, he was chosen by Joe to be chained in prison.

We'll finish this chapter next time. Gotta finish moving Jody and kids in next couple days. So, until next time Keep lookin' up.

Blessings, Mike

Joseph is Generous to His Brethren, but Simeon is in Chains, and Jacob Won't Give Benjamin Up

Afternoon folks. Got Jody's apartment moved out and put in storage till she can move into the house she bought (maybe next week). Not too cold here in Fairbanks, AK. but snow on the ground and it won't melt till spring. I'll be here till Dec. 1st. Then back to MN., then drive to AZ. Well, let's see if we can finish this chapter. God has things moving to complete his prophecy in Genesis 15:13. (What He says will always be.)

Let's pray.

Genesis 42:25–38 KJV

I. A time of panic for the brothers.

A. Verses 25 to 28. This is a well-traveled trade route from Egypt to what will later be called Babylon, and there were roadhouses along the way about a day's travel apart. There may have been stretches of this route they may have had to camp, not sure, but there were many roadhouses along the way. Back in the old-time days in Alaska, roadhouses were strung out along all the trails between Dawson City, Yukon Territory, Canada and Fairbanks, Alaska. One didn't have to camp much. Likewise, in Mongolia, there were many roadhouses where one could get something to eat and roll out your sleeping bag for the night. (Good old days, miss 'um!) Anyway, they stop for the night. They had to feed their livestock so imagine the shock finding one's money he bought the grain with back in one's sack! What's going on! Are they going to be framed, or what? They truly see all the things that happened to them as punishment for their wickedness to their blood brother. Verse 28. What has God done to us! I still don't know which of 2 Corinthians 7:10 they have, true repentance or just that they are reaping what they sowed and now are caught.

II. They make it home with their loaded mule train.

A. Verses 29 to 35. They explain to their father what happened to them, which we already know. But then they found their money in all their sacks, and again they're thinkin' we're in trouble now, we have to go back to Egypt. Now, will they all be thrown into prison? What to do? They know this is a punishment from God.

III. The difference between Jake and Joe.

A. Verses 36 to 38. Here Jake is acting as one not born again, holding onto all the knowledge of the promises of God and the proof of all He has done for him in the past. Jake seems to forget. Whereas Joe, when handed lemons in his life, he continued on. This is God's working grace in Joseph and leaving Jacob to be miserable and blaming the sons he has from his other wives. He's leaving God out of all this, trying to sort things out on his own. We know Romans 8:28, but I know there have been times in my life I've acted just like Jake. (Although I do remember a time or two I acted like Joe. It was God who enabled me to, not myself.) It seems to take God to remind us to trust him; He's got a plan. Elijah is a good example of this both ways. (1 Kings 18,19) Jake will still make the Faith Hall of Fame but only for what he did just before he died. I personally don't think much of him in his life. The way he treated his sons was not good. But even then, God is directing for His purpose.

1. Verse 38. This chapter ends with "no!" Benny is not going! I will grieve too much when he is lost to me! Even at the promise of Reuben saying you can kill my sons if I don't bring him back. God is not in Jake's thoughts at this point. But soon he will have to send Benny down cause starvin' times are upon them.

This is a short one, but a good study and as always, we should consider ourselves in applying this to our lives.

Blessings, Mike

Questions for Discussion – these concern the last two studies.

1. Considering Joe in verses 23 and 24 – seems even though what they did to him could well make him hate them to vengeance, he still loved them. Is that a natural way for man? Or how was he able? Consider yourselves.
2. How about Jake? Both were believers. I wonder what it would take for us to deal rightly with a tragedy like this? Use the Bible to answer.

Joseph's Younger Brother is Brought to Him as He Requested

A bag of grain will last only so long. Mornin' folks. It's -10 F this mornin' in Fairbanks, AK. The grandkids are keepin' me busy runnin' "Poppas Taxi," and we'll be taking Jody's things out of storage and moving them into the house she bought. Start that this coming Friday.
Well, it's now the Tuesday after and we've moved her in with the help of a bunch of my oldest grandson's buddies. So now I'm able to finish this study, Praise the Lord. It's been hard to get much studying done. We'll be heading to Arizona Dec. 1st via Minnesota to pick up our car. Might not get another done till we get down there.

Let's pray!

Genesis 43:1–34 KJV

I. A bag of grain will last only so long, and the drought outlasts the bag!

    A. Verses 1 to 10. Jake is hoping things would change and the rain would come before they'd run outta grain. Didn't happen. So now he says, you'd best go for some more; we're almost out. Ignoring the fact without taking Benny they won't get grain. Verses 1 and 2.

        1.   Verses 3 to 5. Judah seems now to take the reins from Reuben as head son and tells his Ol' Pa the way things sit concerning buying grain in Egypt.

Without Benny going with us, there will be NO GRAIN! Therefore, we won't bother going down, and we'll just have to starve like the poor of this land are!

2. Verse 6. God starts working in Jacob's heart. He's called Israel now. He's going to shortly recognize there is a true, sovereign God that he worships. But here he strikes back at his son, blaming them for having to take Ben down there to Egypt.

3. Verse 7. The boys stand up to their father and say, how would they know that "Head Man" of Egypt would demand their little brother for more grain? (Good question for which Israel doesn't have an answer.)

4. Verses 8 to 10. Judah again takes charge and says he'll take full responsibility for Benny getting back safely to their father, but we must take him, or we'll not get any grain! You can even kill my little ones if it makes you feel better! Fact is Pa; we'd be back by now if you'd have let us take Ben down but now, you'll be hungry for a while!

B. Verses 11 to 14. Here Israel stops trying to go it alone and submits to the fact God is in control of this as He is in all things.

1. So, he surrenders to the cold, hard facts. He has no choice but to trust God and says go with the money you found in the bags of grain as well as enough to buy grain again and some things they don't grow in Egypt. But most important is he surrenders Benny to go.

2. Verse 14 shows Israel is starting to think right. Basically, the Lord's will be done and give back

Simeon, as well as Benny. Or if he doesn't, so be it!

II. So they go and come with Benjamin and stand before Joseph. Now what?

A. Verses 15 to 23. So off they go. and in one verse they are in Egypt. It seems the closer they get, the more fear they feel. What is this Egyptian up to? Then Joe sees them and Ben with them. It doesn't say, but you can imagine what his heart feels like. He plays his cards close to his vest, not letting anyone know these are his brothers. I'd say this would take some self-control. According to James 3:2, Joseph is a perfect man. He tells his head butler to bring them all to his house to eat dinner with him, which he does.

1. This really puts fear in the brothers. Verse 18. They pulled up close to the head butler and told him of the money found in their feed sacks. Verses 19 to 22.

2. Their fears are relieved. Verse 23. Relax, Boys! Your God, the God of your fathers, has blessed you! I put the money in your sacks. (I wonder if they're thinkin' about how careless they have been to their God and yet He's with them?) Then that bloody son of Jacob, Simeon, appears to them all the brothers are together. Yet the one brother who prophesied to them is about to appear and that prophecy is about to come to pass. But first, they are treated like proper guests. Verse 24. They get out the gifts for this strange Egyptian before they are to eat with him. Verse 25.

III. The Prophecy fulfilled.

A. As God says it will be, it will. God spoke to this family through Joseph over twenty-two years ago that this day would come and now in this verse 26, it happened. "They bowed themselves down to earth" to him.

B. Verses 27 and 28. He asks them how it is with their Ol' Pa, and they tell him. Then in verse 29, he looks on his full, little brother and asks a blessing on him. But as one could expect, Joe has to quickly go to get by himself to let out the emotions that were swelling up inside him. All these years of waiting, taking the suffering and sorrow, and shame and then to lay his eyes on his little brother would bring this about. As yet, the time isn't right to reveal himself to his brethren. Verse 30. He is still not done with their trial to be sure their repentance is true. The self-control Joseph has truly is from God as his faith in trusting God would eventually fulfill what he said He would. So, Joe holds his tongue (James 3:2) mature in faith. Amazing testimony. I'm sure I would have failed alone, and only by the Grace of God can one have this wisdom which is from above. (James 3:17)

1. They fellowship and eat. But Egyptians won't eat grub with Hebrews, and Joseph doesn't want his brothers to know him yet. He eats alone on one table, his brothers on another, and the Egyptians at another. They seemed to have a good time. But with one peculiar thing; he placed the brothers in order of their age and then gave his little brother a whole lot more than the other brothers. How did this strange Egyptian know this, the brothers thought? Verses 31 to 34.

We've still got another chapter of trials for these brothers to go through before Joe will reveal himself to them. Probably won't get to it till we're in AZ. Thanksgiving is upon us, and with that, we ought to be thankful that He didn't give us what we deserve, but gave himself in our place! Thank you, Lord!

Blessings, to ya all! Mike

The Final Test

Hi ya'all! We're in AZ. Finally. Long time in the saddle! We whipped and spurred getting down here and thank the Lord we got here safely. Still a little tired. Well, we're getting close to Joe revealing himself to his brothers but not quite ready. One more test to see how they will respond.

Let's pray.

Genesis 44:1–34 KJV

I. They had a good time, but now it's time to go and get this grub back to their hungry family, but Joseph has another plan.

A. Verses 1 to 6. The plan is to bring them back with fear and regret. The Cup of Joseph was a cup of silver, this and similar cups were used by many of the Occult to see into future (or try). These Hebrews were still thinking this Egyptian had such powers (not yet knowing he's their brother that trusts in the God of Abraham). So, Joe's head servant does as he's told, then takes off after the brothers to accuse them, find the cup, and bring them back to Joe. Which we see he does in verses 7 to 12. They, of course, had no idea the cup would be there, (the cup would be in Benny's sack) and they state how honest they were with this Egyptian. They, knowing there couldn't be the cup in any of their sacks, quickly take down the sacks and, of course, the cup is right where the servant put it. So now what?

II. They know God is behind all this and know this is all happening because of their sin.

A. Possibly this test is bringing out the character of the brothers. Perhaps they will just figure to be rid of this other favorite son of their father, even if it kills their father. So what? We'll divide what he has. Or will they act with righteous sorrow and fear?

1. Verses 13 to 16. They tear their clothes, all of them (those days a sign of grief). They show a righteous response, for instead of saying tuff luck Benny, ya got caught now ya gotta pay up; we're going home, they're worried about Benny. As we'll see also, they are worried about their father, but most of all we see they're truly sorry for their sin, knowing the true God is punishing them. They as well seem to have true repentance, verse 16, and commit themselves to Joseph as his servants to do to with them as he pleases.

2. But Joseph says no. Only the guilty one (Benny) will serve me. You all can go home (this too is a test).

3. Judah then recites all that has happened, verses 18 to 31, and how if Benny doesn't go home their father will die of a broken heart.

4. Then Judah pleads that he take Benny's debt of sin himself, be a bondservant, and Benny goes to their father, verses 32 to 34, for he gave his father his word that Benny will return to him. Verse 34. Judah truly has the right motives shown for he confesses he cannot bear to see his father mourn at the grave for the loss of both his favored sons. Please take me for the payment of the wrong

done to you. (Reminds me of the ONE who bore my sin debt so I could live.)

In the above, I think of not only myself concerning the self-shame that comes when recognizing guilt from sin, but also the relief from confession and forgiveness. David comes to mind in Psalms 51:15-17; 17 being the important part. A soul in deep sorrow over their sin, such as David was. It seems a contrite one who is humbled by the truth of recognized sin, and he sees he is not self-sufficient but needy of not only forgiveness but Grace to be righteous. This and only this will God accept. In Psalms 51:7–14, we see that broken and contrite heart of David confessing that brings relief and joy to a sinner such as me. Notice too in verse 13, where others will see the way to be right with God. Likewise, later is a picture of this with the brothers from Joseph.

Well, it didn't take long to get through this chapter but a good application for us. Blessings to you all this time of year when we remember the appointed time for the "Seed of the Woman" to become a man to make man right with Him.

Merry Christmas, Mike

Question for Discussion

1. When confession comes from us to God and for-giveness comes from God to us, then relief comes, correct? "Contrite heart" has to do with something broken. What? James 4:6 might help.

Surprise! I'm Your Little Brother Joey!

Morning folks. I've been preaching some last couple weeks so now we'll see if in the next five to six weeks we can get Genesis finished.

Let's pray.

Genesis 45:1–28 KJV

I. I'm your brother Joseph you sold into Egypt.

A. Verses 1 to 4. This is the beginning of the 400-year "Sojourn" in Egypt that God intended for Israel to go through. This was told to Abraham in Genesis 15:13, and the only reason God gave Abe was in Genesis 15:16. Nevertheless, God has a purpose that He intended to accomplish even though to us, we might question it. (Isaiah 14:24) What is interesting is the abundance of the gift of grace God gave to Joseph. We need to remember all these things that were said previously were handed down, they weren't forgotten (like Genesis 15:13), with the information and knowledge of God's ultimate plan for "redemption" the measure of the gift of grace (ultimately through Christ, Ephesians 4:7) for the purpose God has for that individual to accomplish. Here Joseph was given a powerful amount of faith as well as wisdom to use the knowledge he had of the Holy One. This is how Joe was able to stand the trials he was given. Now comes the time to let his brothers know: "It's me!" It was emotional for Joseph, but frightening for the ten older brothers. Verse 3. "Were troubled" is putting it lightly, THEY WERE TERRIFIED! To make it worse verse 4, but then he explains to them what partially eases their fears.

1. Verse 5 explains God, in His plan, was using them in their bitterness and hatred for Him to get Joe in Egypt to prepare a place for them to "preserve life." I still see an example of Christ to us in Joseph toward his brothers, in that when we were yet sinners, Christ died for us. (Romans 5:8) Joe suffered for them and did the will of God to save them and forgave them! The famine is indeed a killer; people can't live without water and food. Sudan is a recent example of this. I'm sure the population of Canaan was thinned out badly at that time. Then in verse 6, Joe says there are five more years of this drought; many people will die.

2. Verses 7 and 8 expound further for the brothers to understand, this ALL was God's doing. Yet, they were the evil force God used to accomplish it. They, in the last chapter, finally recognized their guilt by the test Joe put them through. But truth is, Jacob had a lot of responsibility for what they had become. His selfish love created the evil in them. Nonetheless, this all was God's providence. God placed Joe in this high position in Egypt to protect Israel, "For through you, ALL nations will be Blessed." (Because of the "Seed of the Woman" you are transporting.)

II. Now, go get Ol' Pa and bring him to me!

A. Verses 9 to 24 explain what they are to tell their father, that this truly is Joseph who is before them, verse 12, and how much he truly loves them regardless of what they did to him. Verses 14 and 15.

    1. It seems all of Egypt rejoiced with Joseph when word got out what had happened. Verse 16.

B. Then the Pharaoh gets excited for his good friend and counselor and gives the best of his land to Joe's family, verses 17 to 20, as well as a rich outfit to go and get their families down to Egypt.

    1. Verses 21 to 24. So, Joe outfits his brothers as the Pharaoh said and sent them to get Ol' Pa. He gives them cloths and silver and Benny gets five times what the others get, and the best kind of grub one could have on the trail. All this suffering by both Joe and Jake, as well as guilt by the brothers, turn out for the good, and so they head home.

III. Pa! Joey's alive and is the Prime Minister of Egypt! He tells you to light a shuck for Egypt! (Come a Runnin!)

A. I'm thinking it must have been more than a little tuff to tell their Pa what they did to their little brother, but now he's got the power in Egypt to give them all they could ever dream of having! Verses 25 and 26. This is hard for Jake to believe till he saw the outfit the Pharaoh sent for him to travel with, then he believed. Verse 27.

B. Verse 28. Let's go see my Beloved Son!

God's story is truly an amazing story, and this is just one part of His-Story.

Have a Blessed Christmas and be thankful, Mike

A thought to consider: God foretold this move to Egypt would happen to Abe back in Genesis 15:14. Now it has happened. Over and over, He tells man ahead of time what is going down, and then it comes to pass. It seems this should tell us who's in control and give the "free will" philosophy a problem.

Jacob Makes the Big Move to Egypt and God's Final Visit with Jacob

Mornin' folks. Hope ya all were blessed this Christmas. 2016 is four days away. Worldwide there are many challenges and dangers. Yet, our God is well aware of them all and we know nothing will happen outside His plan, His-Story. Romans 8:1 promised we can face them with confidence.

Let's pray.

Genesis 46:1–34 KJV

I. Jacob starts out for Egypt but first makes a stop where he grew up, Beersheba.

A. Verses 1 to 4. He gets to Beersheba and goes to the place they offered sacrifices before and offered to the "God of his father, Isaac." I find it interesting it doesn't say, God of Abraham, as well as Isaac. It may refer to Genesis 17:19 because the promise or covenant was through Isaac and passed to Jacob.

1. Verses 2 and 3. Nonetheless, this is God's last time speaking to Jacob. Why God doesn't address him as Israel, I'm not sure. Even later, after Israel is a nation, He will, when speaking to them say, "I AM the God of Jacob." Perhaps He is recognizing Jacob as the father of Israel the Nation. When he wakes up, God tells him his journey to Egypt

will go well, and Joseph will be at his side when he dies (closes his eyes). This is the eighth and final time God speaks to Jacob.

II. He starts out with the assurance of God's blessings. Verses 5 and 6. But now we see the list of names of the sons of Jacob.

A Jacob rises up and gets in the wagons the Pharaoh provided cause of being Joseph's father. He's too old to ride a camel or walk. He, along with all the little ones, are in the wagons. Can't help, as an old stockman myself, wondering what kind of shape the stock was in. Three years into the drought, sure cuts the growth of the grass. It doesn't say.

B. Then we get to verses 7 to 27 that all list the boys of Jake, along with their sons. So, we'll list them here now.

    1. Leah had six sons. Verses 8 to 15.
        a. Reuban - four sons
        b. Simeon – six sons
        c. Levi - three sons
        d. Judah, who is now the leader – five sons
        e. Issachar – four sons
        f. Zebulun – three sons
        g. Along with Leah's daughter, this family of Jake's, counting Dinah is 33. God killed Er and Onan, making 29 but then in verse 12 we see Pharez had two sons so now we're back up to 31 souls. Now probably Leah had another daughter that wasn't mentioned so count Leah for 33.
    2. Verses 16 to 18. Then comes Leah's handmaid, Zilpah.
        a. Gad had a slug of boys – seven

> b. Asher – four sons,
>
> c. and one of these sons, Beriah, had two sons, as well as Asher, had a daughter, Serah. So, 16 altogether.

3. Verses 19 to 22. Then we come to Rachel, the one Jake lusted after, whose womb God didn't open for a long time.

   a. Joseph had two sons in Egypt

   b. Benjamin had lots of boys (as God intended) – ten sons

   c. Rachel gave Jake 14 souls.

4. Lastly, Bilhah, Rachel's handmaid. Verses 23 to 25.

   a. Dan had one son, Hushim

   b. Naphtali had four sons

   c. Seven souls altogether.

5. So, I count 65 including the four wives and Jake, but here in verse 26 it says 66, so someone isn't named, probably a girl. Also includes Joe and his kids, so must have been some girls born that weren't mentioned, or maybe servants. Oh, I forgot Rachel had died. Remember? My version (KJ) in verse 26 says "besides" Jacob's sons and wives, all were three-score and six = 66, which leaves room for some girls maybe. Also, Benny was still a kid at this time, so his kids aren't there yet.

III. The meeting of Jacob and Joseph back from the dead.

A. Verse 28 tells us that Jake is now depending on Judah to be the responsible one and sends him to get directions to Goshen. He goes and sees Joe to find out just where they should go. Wagons move slowly so with a fast camel he could go to Joe and come back to meet them and guide them to Goshen.

B. In the meantime, Joe is anxiously preparing to go to Goshen himself to see his father. (Verse 29) When he gets there, it is a great renewing time with lots of love and tears. Then in verse 30, Jake says now I'm satisfied with this life for I've seen my beloved son who was dead to me, but now I find him alive! I'm ready to die! But he doesn't die yet.

1. Verses 31 to 34 explain how Joe needs to go back and tell the Pharaoh Jake has come to him. I'll tell them you're an Old-Time Stocker, meaning they mostly run cows; which they do run some. (Not necessarily sheep men cause they, like the old-time ranchers here in the U. S. of A., thought sheep men were lowlifes that don't deserve to be on the range.)

2. Then he goes on to say you'll have to come before the Pharaoh and you'll have to explain who you are as to your life's trade. You'll say it so he'll see you as cattlemen for sheep men are lower than dirt to Egyptians.

a. We need to remember that when Joseph came to Egypt, the Dynasty was called "The Shepard Kings." If you remember back to studying when Joe was brought to Egypt in chapter 39, we saw some invaders, the Hyksos, who were advanced in the bronze culture and had learned to use chariots for warfare, come in and temporarily conquer Egypt. They were more than likely half-breed Semites, so they accepted Joseph more comfortably than if they had been pure Egyptians. There's still a question if they were really shepherds or not, but nonetheless, to Egyptians sheep men weren't wanted as neighbors.

C. Now Israel is in Egypt and, as we saw in Genesis 15:13, they stay there for 400 years.

Think of this, 400 years from now it will be the year 2416! That's a long time. Many generations will live and die there, not ever seeing the promised land. Yet to God, a thousand years is but a moment.

Have a Blessed New Year, Mike

Jacob Meets the Pharaoh; the Starvin' Times Direct the Policies and an Oath is Given

Mornin' folks. Gonna try and knock Genesis out this month; we'll see how it goes.

Let's pray.

Genesis 47:1–31 KJV

I. Israel meets the Pharaoh and is welcomed.

A. Verses 1 to 6. We see the steps of Egyptian Pro-ta-call.

1. Verse 1. Joe goes to the Pharaoh to announce his family, who the Pharaoh invited and provided with wagons and goods to come to Egypt, are here in the land of the River Nile's "delta" area called Goshen.
2. Next, in verse 2, he brings in five of his brothers to the Pharaoh and introduces them to him. (It doesn't say who.)
   a. Verse 3. As Joe told his family what to expect the Pharaoh to ask, the Pharaoh does ask, "what do ya do to make a livin'? What's your trade?"
   b. Verses 3 and 4. They tell him they're herdsmen as all their forefathers before

them were and only came to Egypt cause the drought was so bad. We'd lose our livestock, and then we'd all die, so we needed to come to where a river ran good enough to support the grass. We don't want to move here but just wait till this drought passes. Then we'll go home. (I know in the back of their minds the prophecy of Genesis 15:13 is there. 400 years they'll be here which means perhaps 5 or 6 generations.

   c. Verses 5 and 6. The Pharaoh seems happy for Joe and says, "Give them the best grassland for their stock, and by the way, perhaps I could hire them to manage my herd."

B. Verses 7 to 12. Whether it is right away or a little later isn't clear, but nonetheless, lastly, Joe brings Ol' Pa to meet the Pharaoh. Here's what is a God-inspired meeting. Really, all things are God-inspired, some are more noticeable than others. (Isaiah 14:24) Ol' Pa is a chosen vessel by God, and it seems the Pharaoh was the greatest King in that part of the world at that time. Pharaoh recognized this man is a Priest of these Hebrew's God. The God that used Joseph to give the meaning of his dream concerning the drought. He submitted to being blessed by the man of God, Jacob. Much like Abraham being blessed by Melchizedek back in Genesis 14:19 (the Greater always Blesses the lessor). While Jacob was FAR from being poor, this is a good reminder wealth will never be a factor in who is determined superior in God's Story. We don't know all that was said in this meeting, but I'm sure much more than we read here.

1. In verse 9, notice the word pilgrimage. If we compile all the spoken promises from Genesis 3:15 to here and realize these weren't forgotten but recorded, as well as realize there was more that wasn't recorded, we then can see these Elect of God knew and had a great faith which produced a solid hope. (Confidence in what God promised them.) It should bring us to understand the depth of what they understood about where their REAL home was, hence when we read Hebrews 11:8–16; we can understand a deeper picture of their faith. They were men much like us that did struggle with things they faced in this life. Yet, by grace, they believed even in the times when they failed to completely trust God in their life's disappointments and temptations. Then once again to me, Joseph stands out as one who stood in faith through trials. From what I can see, God gave him a large dose of grace in faith in the things promised his father and those before him like Abraham, Shem, Noah, and so on. He stood on the Promises of God!

2. Here is recorded the age of Jacob: 130-years-old. He recognizes his life had some tuff times, but through them, God provided. Abe was 175-years-old when he died, and Isaac was 180-years-old. Jake will live 17 more years.

C. Verses 11 and 12. We see how God used Joseph to prepare the way that ensures Israel, God's chosen people, the Nation whereby all nations will be blessed, their survival. They are in a well-watered place where the grass, even in the drought was good. They have the Pharaoh's blessing, and Joe can be sure his family has enough to eat. My, what a story to bring this prophecy to come to be!

II. The drought continued, and Joseph saves the people.

A. Verses 13 to 26 are a step by step worsening of the drought. Yet, thanks to God through Joseph, the people were saved. The following is what went down.

1. Verses 13 and 14. The people paid for the grain, but still, the drought continued.
2. Verses 15 to 17. The people had no money, so they came begging for food. By the wisdom of God, Joe was changing the whole system to make the Pharaoh rich, yet save the people as God intended. Joseph said, sell me your livestock for food. Then the Pharaoh owned all the stock, but the drought continued.
3. Verses 18 to 20. Now then the people again came to Joe with a deal they agreed to in verse 19. They ask him to buy them, and their land, and they will serve the Pharaoh. It's either this or starve. (This, in my opinion, is a whole lot better than the way our country gives out free food and ruins people to where they think it's their right to be given all that they need at another's expense. Paul said it this way; 2 Thessalonians 3:10–11.)
   a. Verse 21. So, the Pharaoh got them and their land for food. He moved them to cities (this in itself would be a big project), so they could distribute the food, as well as put them to work.
   b. Verse 22 is interesting. This is Egypt's state-run religion. These Priests had a lot of lands and didn't have to give up anything. Of course, this whole religion was an abomination to God, but He will deal with that later.

4. Verses 23 to 26. We see the future plan is explained, and it's a fair one. After the drought is over, you'll go back and work your land. I'll give you the seed (and livestock, I assume to work the land with) and you'll pay me one-fifth of what you grow, and you'll keep four-fifths. (That's like a 20% tax, not a bad deal really and they didn't die in the famine.) So, in verse 26, we see it was made into a law.

III. Israel is settled in the land of Goshen, but as his time is closing, Jacob asks Joseph to make an oath to him.

A. Verse 27 says they stayed in this land Goshen and prospered much, both in livestock and in the numbers of their family's growth. A footnote in one commentary noted that with the number of their family when they came to Egypt at 70, then at a 5% growth rate it would take 215 years to come up with 2,000,000 in population. That's a large family! God said they'd be in Egypt for 400 years. They didn't leave after the drought was over as the commentator seemed to think. I bet that land of the Nile delta was a very good place to be.

B. Verses 28 to 31. Jacob lives 17 more years, and in his last year (probably) he calls Joseph to him. He knows he's gonna die soon and wants to be buried with his fathers in the land God promised to them.

1. He asks Joe to make an oath, and as Abraham did with his servant to guarantee the oath to get a wife for Isaac from the land Abe was born in, Jacob had Joseph grab hold of his reproductive organs and swear to his father that he'd make sure they'd get his body back to the land they purchased for a family burial plot. Joseph did.

C. Now we see the stage that God set for Israel to come out of Egypt as a Nation. Again, Isaiah 14:24. (I think we tend to forget this.)

Have a great weekend!

Blessings, Mike

Questions for Discussion

1. Read over I.B.1 again in this study. Have you in the past realized the fact that God told all these things that happened starting with Genesis 3:15 concerning God making a way for man to be right with God? All these, God's Elect passed down generation to generation. They knew these promises and believed, but like us, sometimes or maybe often, have trouble with Faith over our circumstances. I question if much of the Church understands how these old-time saints, chosen by God, understood these truths/promises. Do you understand?
2. Concerning Joe's faith, I often fear people seem to think it was the individual that made a decision to believe. Like it came from them. How does Ephesians 2:8 explain where an individual gets his or her faith? Could we then say God enabled me to believe or have faith? "God enabled me," is perhaps a more honest statement than simply saying, "I believe."

The Blessings

Mornin' folks. Three more studies to go. One thing that's come to mind is when Jacob was told that Joseph was killed and Jake went to pieces over this news, he went into Spiritual decline. All that God led him through in the past, as well as blessed him with, was forgotten. He was consumed with sorrow. God didn't wake him out of this till Genesis 43:13–14. Then He revived him in Genesis 45:27–28. True, it all started with the way Jake treated his sons concerning love, in that Joseph he loved more than the others. This led to bitterness to the extent of desiring to have Joe killed. Nonetheless, all that God did and promised seemed to be forgotten, which affected the whole family.

Yet it seemed in Judah however, that God started leading him to repentance. Back in chapter 38, with all that went on with Tamar, it appears God was dealing with his character judgment and Judah started to look at himself honestly and began taking leadership of the family. Then we see in Genesis 44:33, where he was willing to give his life for the sake of his little brother Benny, and his father's life. It's interesting that in this chapter, we see Jacob blessing Joseph's sons. God gives him the order of the Blessings. This is what put Jacob in the "Faith Hall of Fame" in Hebrews 11:21. Also, I must apologize for not realizing in Hebrews 11:22, that Joseph was recognized for his faith in God's promise of going into the promised land as the nation of Israel. I said in an earlier study, how God left him out of the faith chapter. I don't know how many times I've read Hebrews 11 and didn't remember God recognizing Joseph, yet he did so. Pardon my dumb spell. We'll see in chapter 49 that Judah is recognized as the transporter of the "Seed of the Woman."

Let's pray.

Genesis 48:1–22 KJV

I. The end of this life for Jacob is very near.

A. Verses 1 to 6. "It came to pass after these things," pointing back to the oath Joseph gave Jacob to bury him in the family plot in Hebron. So, now the time is very near. Verse 1. Joe takes his sons Manasseh and Ephraim to see his father. Verse 2. So, in the distance, a servant probably, sees the Prime Minister of Egypt's chariot coming, and knowing it's Joseph, let's Jacob know. That encourages Jacob to force himself to sit up for this meeting. Then Joe comes in, verses 3 and 4, and Jacob reminds his son, the son he loves the most, the son God used to save the family, and tells what Joseph knew already but needed for our sake to reaffirm God's promise, that they, Israel, will receive all of Canaan and it will be an EVERLASTING possession. (Even in their absence God's promise wasn't canceled. It was still theirs even during their punishments.)

1. Here now in verse 5, God is showing two of the tribes of Israel, who are Joseph's two sons, they will receive an equal inheritance with Jacob's other eleven sons. When Jake says Joe's two sons "are mine" he means they will get Joe's inheritance. Therefore, Joseph's portion is double his brothers'. The eldest son usually gets this, yet the father has the right to change it. Joseph is the firstborn of the wife Jacob wanted, as well as God

used Joseph to save the family.

2. Verse 6. God, through Jake, tells his son Joe that if he has any more sons, they will be part of the "double portion" that is his two sons'. They will both be getting equal portions with Jacob's other eleven sons.

3. Verse 7. Jake recites the sad time of losing Joe's mother when they were traveling down to see Jake's father, Ike. Rachel, his beloved wife, died when they were almost to what is now called Bethlehem.

II. The Blessing.

A. Verses 8 to 16. Jacob didn't wear sunglasses growing old so cataracts scared his eyes more and more till he was nearly blind. I'm sure he was thinking why didn't I use sunglasses more when I thought I was young and tuff. That's a joke. They of course didn't have sunglasses back then. Nonetheless, he saw movement by Joe's legs and asked who's there with ya? Verse 9. Joe's reply is they're my sons. Then the important recognition "that God gave me" here in Egypt before ya came. Regardless how much false religion Joseph was around, God kept Joseph looking to the True God of Jacob all those years. Often wondered about his Egyptian wife, if she ever came to believe in the True God. In verse 10, we see the love of a grandfather here (until ya are one, you'll never know what that special bond is like). He calls them to him and holds them tight for a good long spell. Verse 11. Jake states what he was thinking that he'd never see Joseph again, yet here you stand and not you only, but with my grandsons! God has been SO good to me, even in my lack of faith!

1. Here in verse 12, the blessing begins. Joseph

pushes his sons to his father and bows his head toward the ground. Verse 13. Joseph pushed the boys in such a way that the elder, Manasseh, would be on Jacob's right hand and Ephraim on Jacob's left.

2.   But then Jacob does something strange. Joe's looking down and doesn't see this. Jacob crosses his arms and puts his right hand on the younger and his left hand on the elder! Verse 14 says he did this knowing what he was doing.

a.   In verse 15 Jacob not only blesses Joseph, but also acknowledges with the phrase, "the God that FED me." In Hebrew the meaning seems to point to, "God has shepherded me." This is the first reference to the truth of Proverbs 16:9. You see the sheep doesn't know where the shepherd is taking him. Yet, when he gets to the end of the journey he can look back and see it was the shepherd directing his steps. Here Jacob acknowledges this truth.

b.   Verse 16. The blessing continued. "Redeemed me" by the Angel of the Lord is the first use of this phrase in the Bible, meaning none other than Christ before he became man. "Redeemed me from all evil," is declaring his faith in the promise of the "Seed of the Woman," Christ our Lord and Savior. He paid the debt for our sin. His confidence in what God promised him as to his fathers and with that asks the blessing; Joseph's double portion with his two sons.

III. The order of the Blessing of his two sons troubled Joseph.

A. Verses 17 to 20. Here again, grace reverses the order of nature. If we start back from Abraham's sons Ish and Ike, we see the younger was blessed. Then Isaac's sons Esau and Jacob, again the younger was blessed. Jacob's son Reuben was passed over for Joseph gets the double portion and Judah becomes the "Seed of the Woman" transporter. Later, Jesse's youngest son is blessed or anointed as King. David is Jesse's youngest. Anyway, that's what God decreed, and that's that! So here, Ephraim, the youngest is first blessed and his tribe will be the largest in population. Jacob blesses them as God intended.

B. Verses 21 and 22. Jacob, really God through Jacob, reassures Joseph that God will shepherd Joe with His plans and he will come again to the promised land, the land of your fathers.

1. Then an interesting thing is said in verse 22. Apparently, Jacob got in a fight with the Amorite and conquered him or them. This gave him a piece of ground not mentioned till now in this one place. Like I said before, Genesis is just an overview of all that went on back then. Much more happened that we aren't told. I'm sure it would have been very interesting. Possibly, in John 4:5 is the piece of ground, but the story isn't told. Joseph's double blessing includes this ground.

Well, thar' ya go! interesting study.
Have a blessed week! Mike

Questions for Discussion

1. Jacob, or Israel, sees here the God the Son who redeemed him and paid his debt for sin. Proverbs 16:9 – God was shepherding him. How about you? Do you see this in your life?
2. Do you understand God's sovereign choice will always be done? Study Romans 9:10–23.

The Good and the Bad Revealed;
Blessings and Prophecy Told

Greetings ya all! Well, 48 chapters down; two to go!

Let's pray.

Genesis 49:1–15 KJV

I. All my sons come and hear what the Lord, through your father, has to say of your future.

   A. Verses 1 and 2 are interesting to my thinking. Boys gather around your Ol' Pa and hear what God says about your character and what will be going on in your and your seed's lives generations down the pike (life's road).

      1. Verse 2. "Hear ye sons of Jacob and harken unto Israel, your father." Many hear but don't pay close attention, but YOU need to hear this and REMEMBER so pay attention! You're the sons of Jacob as well your father Israel, who is the chosen one to start the chosen nation, Israel. Remember all the promises of God. (Knowing this, but say you're one of the generations after 300 years enslaved in Egypt. Would you remember?)

      2. Then he, really God, starts with the eldest and works his way down to the youngest concerning their character and what they can expect.

II. Now we look at what God thinks, as well as Jacob or should we call him Israel, about the twelve sons.

A. Reuben is first. Jake, as would be expected, desired of his firstborn. He'd had high hopes and great expectations for him, yet as sons do, they can prove otherwise and big disappointments and shame. But a father wants a son of whom he could say, that's my son! with pride or should we, as Christians, say with Thanksgiving!

1. Verse 4 gets right to the point. If we remember back when Reuben took Bilhah, who was one of his father's wives to bed (Genesis 35:22), Jake didn't seem to say much at the time, but he did remember (as well as God) and looked closely at Reuben. He couldn't ever seem to take the leadership role, and God explains his character this way: you're unstable as water. I think of a creek that the rains come and it rages out of control, then the dry time comes and no water can be depended on. So is Reuben a truly sad epitaph of one's life. (Yet, even this God is in control of.) Reuben's tribe never amounted to much. There was never a Judge from this tribe. They were the first tribe to say to Moses, "ya know we're herdsmen of cattle and this land is good enough. We don't need to cross over the Jordan. We'll stay here. But we'll send our warriors with ya over there to fight the Canaanites with ya." Reuben lost Jake's blessings as the eldest son.

2. As we've already seen in the last chapter, Joseph got the double blessing, and the leadership was passed to Judah.

3. Simeon and Levi – verses 5 to 7. I'll explain this in my words: sons may my soul not come to the depth of your hateful vengeance and be joined

with you so that my honor turns to shame! Then he reminds them of what they did to Shechem in Genesis 34:25 when they, the sons of Jacob, told him that if he wanted to be joined with them through the marriage of their sister, ALL males have to be circumcised. Then in their helpless state, Levi and Simeon slaughtered all the men, hamstrung their bulls, and took back their sister. (Not to mention they were the brothers who wanted to kill Joseph outright.) So, their curse was explained in verse 7. Therefore, they will not inherit land as the other tribes. Simeon ends up absorbed into Judah. Levi gets no land but will end up with cities scattered throughout Israel. Later, when they stood with Moses against rebellion, would become the tribe of priests who did the worship and sacrifices to God. So, the first three sons didn't turn out too good.

4. Then we come to Judah, the son of repentance of God. (2 Corinthians 7:10) Seems after the episode of selling Joseph, Judah's guilt was such he left the family for a spell. Then was shocked into further judging his own character with the episode with Tamar in chapter 38. Eventually, we see him taking charge of the leadership of the clan. In verses 8 to 12, he receives the blessings.

    a. Verse 8. His leadership – his brothers shall praise him. Also, his father's children shall bow down to him. This was done first in Kings David and Solomon.

    b. He will be victorious over his enemies (including that Jesus the Christ spiritually conquered our enemy's sin, Satan, and death).

    c. Verse 9 is interesting. Seems if the Hebrew students who studied this are right, this prophecy is divided between entering into the promised land and when David was king.

d. "A Lion's whelp . . ." concerning being the first tribe to go, conquer and possess their God-given possession (Judges 1:1) ". . . and then goes up to his mountain satisfied."

e. Those Hebrew students think (and probably so) concerning the prophecy of when Judah, through King David, will join all of Israel and conquer his enemies, "he stooped down, he crouched," means he was ready and able to attack his foe, then "and as an old lion who shall rouse him?" This is pointing to after King David conquered his enemies and united Israel, he rested and had honor in the time of King Solomon. Where for forty or so years it seems, they controlled what was promised Abraham concerning the land area. (1 Kings 4:21; 8:65) Most students think the "River of Egypt is the Nile though some, like me, think the little dried creek, Wadi el-Arish is known as the River of Egypt, and is the south boundary.

f. Then we come to the important part of the prophecy, verse 10, concerning the "Seed of the Woman," our Lord and Savior. The word I key in on, of course, is SHILOH. The Hebrew students old and modern, generally agree to the meaning,"One who Brings Peace." We know the peace he is pointing to is between God and man, and this is the Messiah, the Christ.

g. The first phrase of the verse, "A scepter shall not depart from his hand," is concerning the prophecy for Judah for when the time of the king of Israel comes who will join all of Israel together. Judah will have a king come from King David, and the kingship or scepter shall not depart till Shiloh comes. Well, sir! The northern tribes got runoff by Assyria and were no more. The tribe of Judah was punished by a seventy-year exile but was placed back and was Judah. Then anyone from any other tribe was considered a Jew. They would remain a nation (even if controlled by Rome) "till Shiloh come," meaning Jesus, the lion of the tribe of Judah. (Revelations 5:5) 70-years after he'd risen, Judah was no more. Of course, this is the "Seed of the Woman!" All of Genesis is concerning getting the "Seed of the Woman" transported to the tribe of Judah.

h. Verses 11 and 12 are for me a little tuff to figure which way it's going. Is it toward the Messiah? Or is it about the inheritance of land? Or both? There're parts of the land of Judah that had some of the best fields of grapevines, healthy and strong, and pastures with strong graze for stock. Then, Judah, has the mule eating the vines which represent the other tribes that Judah absorbs. Anyway, we know in John 15:1, He is the vine. We know that wine is also used as an example of the Blood of Christ. So, the grape could be seen as Christ who washed us in His blood, which would be the juice of the grapes. Likewise, the grass was so strong of feed from that rich ground; the milk was fat and plenty, meaning land of plenty. Likewise, white also means clean as without sin. These are some of the meanings and thoughts by many who study deeper than I do into the original languages and translations. But we again stress the importance of the prophecy of "The Lion of the Tribe of Judah," as the promised Savior and Lord of ALL! Now on to the rest of the brothers!

5. Zebulun and Issachar (verses 13 to 15) are full brothers from mother Leah, but they came after Rebecca's handmaid and Leah's handmaid had their sons from Jacob and also their sister Dinah. There's not a lot said about them, so we'll assume they were somewhat as dysfunctional as the ten brothers were. However, some good things were said.

   a. Zeb was mainly the prophecy of where that tribe would hang their hat. Now what it says about it is it would be a "safe harbor" for ships. It is strange if you look on a map describing where they were, it shows they were land-locked. But then you read in Matthew 4:12–17 that it had the Sea of Galilee as part of the boundary. But the important part to understand is Zeb stuck his hand in a bag (so to speak) and drew "lot #3" (Joshua 19:10). This was the boundary of what God intended for him over 400-years BEFORE he drew that lot! This should then give us pause to consider God's control on our lives according to His Sovereign Decree!

b. Issachar was older than Zeb, but was put after rather than before Zeb, possibly cause his lot would end up between Zeb's and Dan's lots, "crouching between two burdens."1 Chronicles 12:32 tells a little more about their nature concerning they had an "understanding of what was important.

c. Verse 15 goes along with what was said in 1 Chronicles concerning wise farming and diligence. The valleys and mountains were rich, and crops and olive orchards were strong.

I think this is enough to chew on. I'll finish the rest of the chapter next time. To me, one of the things that encourage my faith in this study is that He has foretold what shall come to pass! And ALL DID! So, what should that tell us about our lives? He has that already planned out according to His purpose for our part in His-Story. He will get us there. These people were just normal people He raised up to work out what He intended in spite of themselves, and likewise, He will with us. (Philippians 1:6) Till next time.

Blessings, Mike

Questions for Discussion

1. The question for ya is in the last paragraph. What does that do for your faith?

2. The verses 8 to 13 really are the main purpose of this study God impressed on me to do. That is, to connect all the stories in Genesis together to point

to the tribe from whom our Savior would come. All the way from Genesis 3:15 until here, it was leading us to comprehend this: the Wisdom of God, the Power of God and the Orchestrating of God making His-Story as the most creative story there ever was and the only story that is. Again, Romans 11:36. My hope is that I, by God's grace, succeeded in teaching this truth.

Continued Blessing Sons and Burial Instructions

Mornin' folks. Took longer studying what I got done last week so we'll finish up chapter 49 this week, then maybe get chapter 50 knocked out after that. Lotta pages in this study through Genesis: almost a book. I believe it's an accurate study, may be helpful to someone, I hope. It was for me.

Let's pray.

Genesis 49:16–33 KJV

6. Verses 16 to 18. Dan, the son of one of Jacob's concubines, will be a tribe with an inheritance and will be a Judge. That is said in Verse 16. But then the next verse likens Dan to a poisonous snake. There are probably several intentions in this statement concerning prophecy.
   a. Sampson was the judge from Dan, who through trickery and supernatural powers, controlled the Philistines and later destroyed a large number of them. He also was killed. (Judges 13 to 16) Likewise, they moved at least in part to the northern border of Israel where there was much fighting to protect their boundary. Those Philistine "dogs" were right next

door as well before any of them moved north.

b. Sadly, in Judges 18, we see as they traveled north and conquered the Zideonites, they took graven images and became an idolatrous people who stayed that way till Assyria took them out in 733 B.C. In that sense perhaps the thought of Genesis 3:15 concerning the serpent bruising the heal may have been thought of. The tribe of Dan is not mentioned in Revelations 7:4–8 concerning the tribes of Israel in end times. Perhaps they were no more from 733 B.C. Jeroboam, in Dan, set up one of his "golden caves" to worship.

c. Verse 18. After Jacob spoke this prophecy about Dan, he spoke this, "I have waited for Thy salvation . . . Oh, Lord!" Well, he doesn't have long to wait, for shortly after Jake concludes his Blessings to his sons, he gives up the ghost. Sadly (I believe), in today's teachings of the Old Testament, there seems to be a misunderstanding that they did not have the same salvation as we on this side of the Cross. Yet, many had a speaking relationship with our Lord, and from what little is said of what God spoke to them about, it's clear they too were first Born-Again. With their spiritual understanding enlightened, understood much of or perhaps more than we do now. Yet, like us, they had their times of valleys when they struggled with faith and were forgetful as we. Look at Jacob's life. It was full of times when God spoke to him, proved

He'd do what He said, as well as proof of the care God gave him, yet when Joseph turned up missing, thinking he was dead, Jacob acted like one without faith. It wasn't till Joseph was proven alive and in authority in Egypt did God bring Jake to the restoration of faith that he is showing here in chapter 49. Hence, he then with great joy shouts out his faith in the promised salvation Job voiced in Job 19:25–27. As Christ said, "Ye must be Born-Again before you can SEE the Kingdom of God" (use the word understand instead of see to get a deeper meaning of how one sees the things God has for us). Jacob now longs to be in the presence of our Lord, God. Especially with prophesying these bad things concerning Dan and some of his other sons.

7. Verse 19. Gad is the son of Leah's handmaid Zilpah. They were settled on the east side of the Jordan. They fought with the Armonites and Moabites and were the first tribe to cross over the Jordan to fight for the other tribes' inheritance. They were known as men of war. (1 Chronicles 12:8) Sometimes they lost battles but then came back victoriously. They stayed on the land till the northern tribes were taken out by Assyria in 733 B.C., but in Revelations 7:5 they were accounted.

8. Verse 20. Asher has only one verse. It's all about the rich dirt that grows the fattest crops and livestock. The land was from the Carmel River to the northern Israel boundary, about twenty miles, with the Mediterranean Sea all along its coast and was about nine-miles

wide. It was the land where King Solomon had his farm that fed his court. It was also the land where Jesus spent much time. That's all it says, but this was a prophecy of the future land Asher would possess. Again, what our all-knowing God told ahead of time would be, is. (Isaiah 14:24) Zilpah was his mother.

9. Verse 21. Naphtali. Now we jump back to Dan's full brother, their mother being Bilhah. While there's not much in Scripture on Ol' Naph, the old Jewish historians used this verse, as well as the history of this tribe, to recognize them as happy, thoughtful people who spoke well, yet could whip their enemies when aroused. Barak came out of this tribe. (Judges 4) It was again a fat land, a land where crops grew quick. Later this was a large part of what is called Galilee where most of Christ's disciples came from. In that sense, "he giveth GOOD words" could be reckoned. The Gospel is the GOOD WORD.

10. Then we come to little Joey who became hated, betrayed, then Joseph the Prime Minister of Egypt and the savior of Israel. Verses 22 to 26 In verse 22, I can't help but think of John. 15:5. The whole life of Joseph was attached to our Lord, and no matter how bad things got, Joe bore much fruit. Another verse I think of is Nehemiah 8:10, specifically the last part of that verse, "the Joy of the Lord is my Strength!" It was Joe's strength. Then in verses 23 and 24 is a brief history of Joseph's life. He was hated yet, so was Jesus. And as Jesus is the chief cornerstone, Joseph is the picture of or a "type of Christ." (I'm sure there were Egyptians in the Pharaoh's

court who were jealous of him, as well as his brothers were before.) His strength was from God concerning his faith in God and His promises.

a. Verse 25. That Joseph, God has and will bless him, through his children (the blessings of the Breast and the Womb), as well as in "Heaven above," his assurance of Salvation.

b. Verse 26 is saying, "Joseph, my son, I have been blessed far beyond my fathers, as well as what they had I received, and likewise, you too shall have this." Then comes the part that is of eternal value, "Unto the utmost bound of the EVER-LASTING HILLS." The Vulgate Latin version says, "UNTIL the Desire of the Everlasting Hills shall come." This is pointing to the Eternal reward that all who are justified through Christ desire. Jacob is again thinking of the soon to come time that he shall be in the bosom of Abraham: his eternal home. Here God promises a crown for Joseph. (1 Peter 5:4)

11. Lastly, Benjamin, verse 27. Little Benny like a wolf? This was a prophecy that is called blessings, even though one would question why. It seems there were many warnings as to their nature that should be guarded against in several of the sons' blessings. Anyway, this prophecy foretells of a very efficient war machine or killing machine. It was shown in Judges 20, where 26,000 fought off 400,000 in two battles, then lost the last which almost cost the existence of the tribe. If you use this

verse with what the first King of Israel, King Saul, was like, this seems to reveal his nature as well, who was a Benjaminite.

    a. So there ya have the blessings given the sons of Jacob, their father, Israel. We need to remember that these things said in Genesis were not forgotten, otherwise, we wouldn't have them in the Bible. They were probably understood better by them back then than now.

III. Israel gives up the ghost.

A. I remember an old lady of the Village of Eagle. No one knew how old she was, but a picture of her way over in the Northwest Territory of Canada, in a village called Red River of the Arctic, taken in 1884, described her as a young girl. That could mean ten or maybe fifteen. She never learned English. All her children were born in a tent. She was one tuff old lady. I remember trying to talk to her, but she'd say, "No savey," meaning she couldn't understand. Anyway, she died about 1985 give or take a year, can't remember for sure. But the reason Liza, that was her name, comes to mind is that she called her kids and grandkids to her bedside and said some similar things as Jake did (not prophesying). She told them that she was going to die now, closed her eyes, and she did. That really doesn't have anything to do with Jake's death, but I thought of it, so I wrote. Verses 28 to 33 describe what he already told Joseph, he now tells all his sons the same; where to bury him with his wife Leah and his parents and grandparents in the burial site that Grandpa Abe bought from that Hittite fella.

    1.   He swung his feet back on the bed, and his soul left his body to head to the bosom of Abraham. (Luke 16:22; Galatians 3:8–9; 2 Corinthians 12:4) He went to paradise, where he knew his family was with our Lord.

So, we got through chapter 49. It took some reading from other "big thick books" to figure these blessings out, but we got it down. It was interesting to me, and it still always amazes me how what God says beforehand; it always comes to pass. Until next time.

Blessings, Mike

Jacob's Funeral and the Death of Joseph

Mornin' folks. Hope you recognize your blessings today for this is the day that the Lord has made, let us rejoice and be glad in it! I'm looking forward to finishing this book. It's been a good study for me anyway. Thanks for riding along with me. Well, let's see if we can finish this up.

Let's pray.

Genesis 50:1–26 KJV

I. Joseph loved and respected his father's wishes.

A. Verses 1 to 6. We see Joe's love for his father, and also, as God promised Jacob, Joseph would be there to close Jake's eyes, and he did. (Genesis 46:4)

1. We've all probably heard of the Mummies of Egypt, and this Joseph had done to his father. The process took forty days. Egyptians mourn for their dead seventy days, so when all this was done . . .
2. Then Joe needed to get permission from Pharaoh to fulfill his father's request to be buried in his family's burial plot in Canaan. He did it by first asking those in the Pharaoh's Court to ask for him of the Pharaoh's permission. The idea is that he'd come back and not stay gone for both he and

his family have proven productive and important to the Pharaoh and would be a great loss. So, to ensure this, the children of Joe's family and their livestock would stay in Egypt. Verse 8.

3. So, the Pharaoh agreed. Verse 6.

II. A caravan is made to take Israel's body to be buried in Canaan.

A. Verses 7 to 14. Now, this was a huge caravan. The Court of the Pharaoh had to be protected, so they had a large contingent of Calvary as escorts, as well as the family of Jacob. Verse 9 says, "a very great company." Now it seems they took the route that would take them east of the Dead Sea, then north to where they'd cross the Jordan River. Why they went this way is not said but if they told us I'm sure it would have made sense. Also, it seems the Egyptians didn't cross the Jordan, which is interesting, but the sons carried Jacob over the Jordan. Verse 13. A caravan that big with chariots and wagons as well as horses would make for a dusty trip. Hopefully, they had a crosswind to blow the dust away from those behind.

1. They got to a place called, "The Threshing Floor of Atad," where for a week they cried their eyes out. It appears the respect was not that Joseph the Prime Minister's father died but Jacob, after seventeen years in Egypt, was recognized as one who held influence over the Pharaoh (remember he blessed the Pharaoh in Genesis 47:10) nonetheless, he seemed to be highly respected. A threshing floor was always on a height of land so the wind would blow the chaff away from the heavier grain that would fall on the floor. The Canaanites were so impressed with this that they

called it, "The Meadow of the Egyptians." (It's also possible that Egypt controlled this area as well.)

2. Verses 12 to 14. The sons kept their word to their father and carried him to the plot of land their great-grandpa Abe bought, and where Abe, Sarah, Ike, Rebecca, and Leah were all buried near Abe's old stompin' ground, Mamre. Which was named after his Ol' buddy Mamre who went with Abe to fight the Kings of the North way back in chapter 14. He'd bought this land from a Hittite fella named Ephron. Nonetheless, the land promised Abe, Ike, and Jacob, they were buried in, and over 440 years later the Nation of Israel shall come here and take the land from a nation God didn't like. Then Joseph and his brothers went back to their homes in Egypt.

III. Last days of the one God used to save Israel: Joseph.

A. Verses 15 to 21. Joseph's brothers (whether Jacob really told them to say this or not, don't know) in fear, confessed they did evil to Joseph, verse 17, and asked for forgiveness. In verse 18, they fell down before him and declared Joseph their master as he had prophesied they would back in chapter 37. Verse 19 caught my thoughts. Joseph is confessing here that he is not in control, but God, the God of Abraham, Isaac, and Jacob had providence over all that went on to get Joe to the position that he held in Egypt. God did it for their good regardless of how much back in chapter 37 they hated Joseph. That hatred was used by God to bring all this to come to pass. Verses 20 and 21. Ya know as we look at this book of Genesis, we should remember all the times God said beforehand what he intended to have happen and it HAPPENED! I hope we may come to realize that what happened isn't about decisions individuals made but what God thought and purposed. The verse that I'm like a broken record with, Isaiah14:24, makes this so clear. We can plan and plan, but what will happen is God will direct our steps to what He has already decreed. (Proverbs 16:9) This truly is His-Story that He authored. In closing this page of His-Story what He intended He accomplished, and that is:

1. Get the "Seed of the Woman" to be carried by the Tribe of Judah.
2. Israel, with his people, is now in Egypt as God foretold where 400 years later, they will come out of Egypt as the Nation of Israel.
3. We watched God giving grace to Joseph to be able to hold in faith all the promises that God had given to his forefathers, regardless of what befell him. God, when Joseph was handed sour lemons and painful things happened to him, allowed him through grace to make lemonade out of those hard times; he never wavered. You see all these promises handed down and told over and over were not forgotten by those who were Born-Again to be in the line of the woman. Eve's Seed and not the Seed of the serpent, Satan, (Genesis 3:15) and of those chosen by God, all had their moments of forgetfulness. Yet, as we look at Joseph's life, we see one who seemed to hold fast to God's promises and with grace had the wisdom to know what to do with this knowledge of the Holy One. As for us, we can look at Romans 15:4 and

understand in whom we should have confidence.

B. Verses 22 to 26. Joseph lived to be 110-years-old and was able to see and hold his grandkids to the third generation.

1. He reminded them that God indeed would bring them out of Egypt to the promised land. Verse 24. He made them take an Oath that his bones would be taken with them when they went (by then perhaps 350-years later). We see again this was handed down generation to generation till in Exodus 13:19, Moses took Ol' Joe's bones with them. So, Ol' Joe went to the city he longed for. (Hebrews 11:16)

What I hope you'll understand clearly through this study is, before the foundations of this world, God planned His-Story out in the pages of His mind as look at this, "The Trail of the Seed of the Woman." Consider 1 Peter 1:18–20, especially verse 20, "ordain before the foundations of the world." The way for man to be made right with God was established.

I hope you, as I, through this study learned to look at Scripture a little differently than before and realize it's not up to the choices man made along the way, but was clearly by the providence of God ALONE. We finished Genesis after about 2 and 1/2 years! This turned into a book.

Blessings to ya all, Mike